Alan S. Cole

A supplemental descriptive catalogue of tapestry-woven and embroidered Egyptian textiles

Acquired for the South Kensington Museum, between 1886 and June 1890

Alan S. Cole

A supplemental descriptive catalogue of tapestry-woven and embroidered Egyptian textiles
Acquired for the South Kensington Museum, between 1886 and June 1890

ISBN/EAN: 9783741177835

Manufactured in Europe, USA, Canada, Australia, Japa

Cover: Foto ©Thomas Meinert / pixelio.de

Manufactured and distributed by brebook publishing software
(www.brebook.com)

Alan S. Cole

A supplemental descriptive catalogue of tapestry-woven and embroidered Egyptian textiles

DEPARTMENT OF SCIENCE AND ART
OF THE COMMITTEE OF COUNCIL ON EDUCATION,
LONDON, S.W.

A

SUPPLEMENTAL DESCRIPTIVE CATALOGUE

OF

TAPESTRY-WOVEN AND EMBROIDERED EGYPTIAN TEXTILES.

ACQUIRED FOR THE

SOUTH KENSINGTON MUSEUM

Between 1886 and June 1890.

BY ALAN S. COLE.

LONDON:
PRINTED FOR HER MAJESTY'S STATIONERY OFFICE,
BY EYRE AND SPOTTISWOODE,
PRINTERS TO THE QUEEN'S MOST EXCELLENT MAJESTY.
AND SOLD AT THE SOUTH KENSINGTON AND BETHNAL
GREEN MUSEUMS.
1891.

Price Sixpence.

CONTENTS.

SUPPLEMENTAL CATALOGUE OF TAPESTRY-WOVEN AND EMBROIDERED EGYPTIAN TEXTILES ACQUIRED BETWEEN 1886 AND JUNE 1890.

(*a*.) TUNICS and ROBES with bands (*clavi*) and square and circular panels (*adjunctæ tabulæ*).

TUNIC (half of) of linen, with narrow shoulder bands, cuff bands, square panels by neck and on skirt, and breast and back ornament, of woven tapestry and needlework, purple wool, and white flax. The ornamentation of the breast and back, between the shoulder bands or *clavi*, consists of rounded arcades beneath which are grotesque Bacchanalian figures. A Greek cross occurs at the centre of neck. The ornament along the shoulder band or *clavus* is of waved stem flanked with ivy leaves and trefoils, and broken at regular intervals by figures of animals. The pattern on the cuff bands consists of acanthus scrolls with flowers and fruits in the open spaces. The square shoulder panel encloses a purple circle picked out with ornament in white outline, within which is a radiating arrangement of four triple branch vine stems. On each of the square panels of the skirt is a group of a lion attacking a gazelle (?). From ancient tombs at Akhmîm (Panopolis), Upper Egypt. *Egypto-Roman.* ? 3rd cent?. 4 ft. 1 in. by 3 ft. 2 in. Bought (242 to 297, 29*l.* 9*s.* 6*d.*). 290.–1887.

The group and attitudes of the lion seizing a gazelle, or goat, in the square panels of the skirt are similar to those frequently used in old and later Persian ornament, as, for instance, in a group of sculpture at Persepolis, in which a lion springs on to a sort of horse, and again in a piece of beaten gold work found at Kertch, possibly of Græco-Scythian work (? 2nd or 3rd cent? B.C.).

TUNIC (child's) of linen, with ornaments, stitched on it, of woven tapestry, brown wool and yellow flax. The pattern on the shoulder bands, which terminate in pendent leaf devices, and on the cuff bands and around the medallions, is of waved stem and vine leaf device. Within the shoulder medallions were representations apparently of human figures; within the medallions on the skirt are rude forms of animals. A portion of the garment is wanting. From ancient tombs at Akhmîm (Panopolis), Upper Egypt. *Egypto-Roman.* 3rd to 6th cent?. 13½ in. by 2 ft. 2 in. Bought, 2*l.* 257.–1890.

4

TUNIC of woven tapestry, green wool with shoulder bands or *clavi* and cuff bands of purple wool, worked in outline with white flax needlework in narrow stripes of small heart-shape, or guilloche devices and small squares filled in with a little circle. Applied to the neck, bottom of skirt, and sleeves of the garment are borderings of red wool worked in flaxen thread with a trellis pattern of small double key devices; and between the openings of the trellis are ornamental star devices. From a cemetery to the north-west of Illahun, near the Fayûm, Middle Egypt. ? 7th cent?. L. 3 ft. 10¾ in., W. 6 ft. 1½ in. Given by H. Martyn Kennard, Esq.

409.–1890.

This tunic is different in style from any other already in the collection.

TUNIC (?) (portion of) of coarse linen, to which has been applied parts of two upright and one transverse band and two square panels of woven tapestry, coloured wool. These are ornamented with large medallions, placed at even distances one from the other and containing debased representations of lions attacking gazelles, and horsemen, singly or in pairs, apparently hunting. Between the large medallions are smaller ones containing nimbed heads of saints, &c. and detached floral ornaments. From ancient tombs at Akhmîm (Panopolis), Upper Egypt. *Christian Coptic.* ? 6th to 9th cent?. About 3 ft. by 3 ft. 3 in. Bought, 1l. 10s.

363.–1887.

TUNIC (portion of), consisting of parts of two shoulder bands (*clavi*) joined by a shorter band across the breast. The shoulder bands are of woven tapestry, flax and coloured woollen thread. The breast band is of blue worsted woven material embroidered in short stitches with white and yellow wool and flax. In the shoulder bands are floral devices, and on one of them is a standing figure of a saint. From ancient tombs at Akhmîm (Panopolis), Upper Egypt. *Christian Coptic.* 6th to 9th cent?. About 12 in. by 9 in. Bought, 5s.

367.–1887.

(b.) BANDS [wide and narrow (*Latus clavus, Angustus clavus*)] for robes, chiefly tunics of the Dalmatic class.

FRAGMENT of a broad band ? of woven tapestry, coloured wools, with part of a nude figure playing a stringed instrument (?) with a bow. Near his head on the right is part of a fish. From ancient tombs at Akhmîm (Panopolis), Upper Egypt. *? Egypto-Roman.* 1st to 6th cent?. About 12 in. by 8 in. Given by Henry Wallis, Esq.

218.–1887.

BAND (narrow, fragmentary) and small MEDALLION, from a child's tunic, of woven tapestry, red wool and yellow flax. The pattern on the band consists of repetitions of small double

scroll devices; that of the medallion consists of a central small
human figure, holding? a bird, set in a circle; beyond and
around it is an arrangement of repeated double scroll devices,
the whole enclosed by an edging of continuous wave ornament. From ancient tombs at Akhmîm (Panopolis), Upper
Egypt. ? *Egypto-Roman.* 1st to 6th cent^y. 9½ in. by 7½ in.
Bought (242 to 297, 29*l*. 9*s*. 6*d*.).   282.–1887.

Compare with similar ornament in No. 1291.–1888.

BAND (fragmentary) of woven tapestry, brown wool and white
flax, for a brown linen tunic. The ornament consists of a
part of two leafy devices between which is a small bird; a
brown panel with a flower, ? a tulip; two brown roundels, one
with a kneeling amorino and basket, and one with a similar
figure holding a bird, in white, and between them, on a white
ground, a brown vase and ? a springing horse amidst delicate
scrolling stem and leaf ornament. Both edges of the band are
of continuous wave pattern. From ancient tombs at Akhmîm
(Panopolis), Upper Egypt. *Egypto-Roman.* ? 1st to 6th
cent^y. 14 in. by 3 in. Bought, 6s.   1340.–1888.

This is noticeable for the counterchanging of the white and brown patterns and
their grounds, and for the fineness of parts of the work.

BAND (portion of) for a linen robe, of woven tapestry, brown
wool and yellow flax. The pattern consists of an alternated
series of two amphora-shaped vases with formal leaf sprigs,
and baskets with similar sprigs. The edge on each side is
of a guilloche pattern outlined in yellow flax with the needle.
From ancient tombs at Akhmîm (Panopolis), Upper Egypt.
? *Egypto-Roman.* ? 1st to 6th cent^y. 2 ft. 3 in. by 2⅜ in.
Bought, 6s.   294.–1889.

PORTION of a breast ornament between the shoulder bands of a
linen tunic, of woven tapestry, chiefly black wool and brown
flax, on which are represented, in black wool, three Bacchanalian figures, two of which are nude, under arcades; along
three sides of it are fragments of rudely rendered ornament,
wave stem and scrolling leaves. From ancient tombs at
Akhmîm (Panopolis), Upper Egypt. *Egypto-Roman.* ? 3rd
cent^y. About 11 in. by 8 in. Bought (242 to 297,
29*l*. 9*s*. 6*d*.).   291.–1887.

Compare this with part of ornament in half of tunic No. 290.–1887. Note also
central figure in this piece, wearing a short sleeve tunic with red and white shoulder
bands (*clavi*).

BAND (fragment of a double) of woven tapestry, brown wool.
The bands are edged with wave ornament. From ancient
tombs at Akhmîm (Panopolis), Upper Egypt. ? 3rd cent^y.
7½ in. square. Bought (994 to 1216, 91*l*.).   995.–1888.

See similar bands in 438.–1889.

BAND (fragment of) for a robe, of woven tapestry, brown wool
and yellow flax, with the figure of a vase. From ancient

tombs at Akhmîm (Panopolis), Upper Egypt. *Egypto-Roman.* 3rd to 6th cent^y. 4¼ in. by 1¼ in. Bought (242 to 297, 29*l.* 9*s.* 6*d.*). 261.–1887.

BAND (part of) for a robe, of woven tapestry in coloured wools and yellow flax thread with pattern of repeated groups of large and small leaf ornament between borders of wave ornament. From ancient tombs at Akhmîm (Panopolis), Upper Egypt. *? Egypto-Roman.* ? 3rd to 6th cent^y. 17½ in. by 1¾ in. Bought (242 to 297, 29*l.* 9*s.* 6*d.*). 262.–1887.

BANDS (portions of two, from a linen robe) of woven tapestry chiefly in red wool and yellow flax. Each band is edged with wave ornament and has on it small white blossoms and coloured tree devices. From ancient tombs at Akhmîm (Panopolis), Upper Egypt). *? Egypto-Roman.* ? 3rd to 6th cent^y. 10½ in. by 4 in. Bought (242 to 297, 29*l.* 9*s.* 6*d.*). 296.–1887.
See also fragments 297, 298, and 298*a*.–1887.

BAND, (part of shoulder and ? breast,) with square panel of woven tapestry on a fragment of a linen robe or tunic, chiefly red wool and yellow flax. On the shoulder band is a vase with trefoil device, a blossom in white, and small tree ornament in coloured wool, on a red ground edged with wave ornament. The breast band is edged with wave ornament on one side, and with stem and ball devices on the other, and between them are small triple-branched plant forms and small ornamental leaves. The square contains a tree ornament in red on acentral white roundel set on square red ground, at one corner of which is a blossom; the whole edged with wave ornament. From ancient tombs at Akhmîm (Panopolis), Upper Egypt). *? Egypto-Roman.* ? 3rd to 6th cent^y. About 8 in. square. Bought (242 to 297, 29*l.* 9*s.* 6*d.*). 297.–1887.
This seems to belong to the robe of which 298 and 298*a.*–1887 are fragments.

BAND, (portion of shoulder) on a fragment of linen, of woven tapestry, chiefly in red wool and yellow flax thread; a vase and trefoil device in white, and small tree ornament in coloured wool are worked on a red ground. From ancient tombs at Akhmîm (Panopolis), Upper Egypt. *? Egypto-Roman.* ? 3rd to 6th cent^y. About 14 in. long. Given by the Rev. Greville J. Chester. 298.–1887.
This seems to belong to the robe of which 297 and 298*a.*–1887 are fragments.

BAND, (portions of shoulder) and border to skirt,? on a fragment of a linen robe of woven tapestry chiefly red wool and yellow flax. The narrow shoulder band has a vase and trefoil device, a small blossom in white, and a small tree in coloured wool on a red ground edged with wave ornament. The skirt border (?) consists of wave ornament next to a broad red band on which are blossom and small tree devices, above which is a stem and ball device repeated, between which are three branched, small plant forms and small ornamental leaves. From ancient tombs at Akhmîm (Panopolis), Upper Egypt. *? Egypto-Roman.* 3rd to 6th cent^y. About 8 in. long. Given by the Rev. Greville J. Chester. 298*a*.-1887.

This seems to belong to the robe of which 297 and 298.-1887 are fragments.

BAND (fragment of, from a child's linen tunic) of woven tapestry (very fine warp and weft threads), coloured silk ; fruits, ducks, and fishes, arranged in small oblong panels, between which is a serpent. From ancient tombs in Egypt. *? Egypto-Roman.* 3rd to 6th cent^y. About 11 in. by ¾ in. Given by C. Purdon Clarke, Esq., C.I.E. 335.-1887.

See square panel No. 334.-1887, which came from the same robe.

BAND (portion of, from a linen robe) of woven tapestry and needlework, brown wool and yellow flax. The pattern on centre of band consists of linked roundels and squares alternated. On each side of it is a wave stem and leaf ornament. From ancient tombs at Akhmîm (Panopolis), Upper Egypt. *?* 3rd to 6th cent^y. 6½ in. by 6½ in. (Bought, 994 to 1216, 91*l*.). 996.-1888.

BAND (portion of, from a linen robe) of woven tapestry, purple wool and yellow flax. The ornament consists of two foliated stems intertwined, and heart-shape leaves repeated in the spaces. From ancient tombs at Akhmîm (Panopolis), Upper Egypt. *?* 3rd to 6th cent^y. 10 in. by 2¾ in. Bought (994 to 1216, 91*l*.). 999.-1888.

BAND (part of) of a robe of rough towel-faced material, of woven tapestry and needlework, brown, green, yellow and red wools and white flax. The ornament consists of a central wave stem bearing vine leaves set between two narrow bands of green and yellow leaf devices. From ancient tombs at Akhmîm (Panopolis), Upper Egypt. *? Egypto-Roman.* 3rd to 6th cent^y. 19½ in. by 5¼ in. Bought, 10*s*. 1306.-1888.

FRAGMENT (probably of breast band for a linen tunic) of woven tapestry, coloured wool, with four panels, in which alternately are seated winged figures holding baskets of fruit and debased rendering of fishes. Beneath this band of panels is a scallop treatment with bowls and vases of fruit, one under each scallop. From ancient tombs at Akhmîm (Panopolis), Upper Egypt. *Egypto-Roman.* 3rd to 6th cent^y. 9½ in. by 3 in. Bought 10*s*. 1308.-1888.

See also 1335, 1335*a*.-1888.

BAND (narrow, round ended, with circular shaped pendant containing a blossom device) of woven tapestry, chiefly red wool and white flax, for a child's robe or tunic. The pattern on the band consists of three divisions, the middle one containing a (?) vase form, from which spring two waved stems, whilst those above and below the middle division contain a series of blossoms and buds alternated. From ancient tombs at

Akhmîm (Panopolis), Upper Egypt. ? *Egypto-Roman*, 3rd to 6th cent^y. 15 in. by 2¼ in. Bought, 7s. 6d. 1321.–1888.

BANDS, (a pair, fragmentary) ? for a linen tunic, of woven tapestry dark blue wool and yellow flax. The pattern of the bands consists of roundels, in each of which is either a plant device or an animal ; in each of the central roundels is a cross worked with the needle in yellow wool. The edges of the bands are of continuous wave ornament. From ancient tombs at Akhmîm (Panopolis), Upper Egypt. ? 3rd to 6th cent^y. 11 in by 6 in. Bought, 7s. 6d. 1329.–1888.

FRAGMENTS, (probably of breast band and one shoulder band to a linen robe) of woven tapestry in coloured wools. The ornament of the horizontal piece (? breast band) consists of a brown border with small pendants forming a series of scallops. On the border are squares and oblongs alternately ; the squares contain floriated crosses, the oblong a double scroll form in red. Under each scallop is a vase of fruit, alternately red and green.* From ancient tombs at Akhmîm (Panopolis), Upper Egypt. *Egypto-Roman*. ? 3rd to 6th cent^y. L. 7½ in. and 4½ in. Bought, 7s. 1335, 1335a.–1888.

* See also 1308.–1888.

BAND, (part of) for a robe, of woven tapestry, coloured wools, with repeated pattern of leaf form and balanced leaf devices. From ancient tombs at Akhmîm (Panopolis), Upper Egypt. ? *Egypto-Roman*. 3rd to 6th cent^y. 6 in. by 1½ in. Bought, 5s. 1344.–1888.

BAND (fragment, for a tunic) of woven tapestry, brown wool and yellow flax. The pattern consists of a degraded representation of a recumbent figure on a brown ground ; on each side of him are repeated double scroll bands with leaf devices. From ancient tombs at Akhmîm (Panopolis), Upper Egypt. ? 3rd to 6th cent^y. 11 in. by 2 in. Bought, 5s. 1349.–1888.

BAND (narrow, part of, from a child's tunic) with pendent trefoil stem of woven tapestry, red wool and yellow flax. The ornament consists of three series of waved stem and blossom device, and a trefoil device between each series. From ancient tombs at Akhmîm (Panopolis), Upper Egypt. ? *Egypto-Roman*. 3rd to 6th cent^y. About 20 in. by 1 in. Bought, 3s. 1372.–1888.

BAND or BORDER with medallion or circular panel of woven tapestry, coloured wool, applied to a piece of coarse brown linen. The pattern of the band consists of repeated small leaf and blossom devices arranged in groups in the style of Egyptian ornament ; between each group is a squared blossom form. The ornament of the circular panel consists of a central roundel and degraded devices about it, surrounded by a broad band, edged with a narrow twisted stem ornament. From an ancient Roman cemetery in the Fayûm, Middle Egypt. ? 3rd to 6th cent^y. 17 in. by 12 in. Bought, 7s. 469.–1889.

Compare leaf and blossom ornament with that in No. 780.–1886.

9

BORDER (? for a linen robe or cloth, small portion) of woven tapestry, brown wool and yellow flax, ornamented with interlacing narrow band or stem patterns, and fringe at one end. From an ancient Roman cemetery in the Fayûm, Middle Egypt. ?3rd to 6th centy. 8 in. by 7½ in. Bought, 2s. 6d.

472.-1889.

See superior specimen of this style of pattern and work in No. 462.-1889.

BAND (round ended), forming a right angle and terminating at one end with a roundel of woven tapestry, coloured wools and yellow flax. The pattern on the band consists of an intertwisting acanthus scroll forming ovals and circles, each enclosing a rosette, a flower, or a bird, on a purple ground. The roundel at one end of the band contains a green cross set in the centre of a red rose with yellow border on a purple ground. ? Egypto-Roman. ?3rd to 6th centy. 22 in. by 16½ in. Bought (with 347.-1890), 12l. 348.-1890.

BAND (fragment of), woven tapestry, coloured wool. The forms are very debased ; ?a lion and part of a four leaf device. From ancient tombs at Akhmîm (Panopolis), Upper Egypt. Christian Coptic. 4th to 6th centy. About 5 in. by 1¾ in. Bought, 5s. 1354.-1888.

BAND (fragment of) of woven tapestry, coloured wools, for a tunic or robe. A rudely represented, but richly draped figure with uplifted hands (praying) is traceable in the fragment, the border of one side only being left. From ancient tombs at Akhmîm (Panopolis), Upper Egypt. Christian Coptic. 4th to 6th centy. 4 in. by 4½ in. Given by the Rev. Greville J. Chester. 1656b.-1888.

BAND (part of the fragmentary pendent panel to a) of woven tapestry, coloured wool. Portions of a rudely rendered crowned and nimbed head, and of a Greek inscription are visible. From ancient tombs at Akhmîm (Panopolis), Upper Egypt. Christian Coptic. ? 4th to 6th centy. About 5 in. by 3½ in. Given by the Rev. Greville J. Chester. 6621.-1888.

BAND (fragment of, for a linen robe) of woven tapestry in coloured wool. From ancient tombs at Akhmîm (Panopolis), Upper Egypt. ? Christian Coptic. ? 4th to 6th centy. L. 14 in. Given by the Rev. Greville J. Chester. 264.-1889.

BAND (small fragment of round ended) of woven tapestry, coloured wools for a linen tunic with debased rendering of two nude human figures, from ancient tombs at Akhmîm (Panopolis), Upper Egypt. Christian Coptic. ?4th to 6th centy. 3¼ in. by 3 in. Bought, 5s. 302.-1889.

BAND (part of, or narrow clavus), with a medallion of woven tapestry, brown wool and yellow flax. The pattern of the band is a waved stem with vine leaf in each wave; that of the medallion, which is edged with small scallops, consists of a small leaf in a central circular band, beyond which is a regular interlaced and looped band with intervening leaves. From ancient tombs at Akhmîm (Panopolis), Upper Egypt. *Egypto-Roman.* 3rd to 7th centʸ. 5 in. square. Bought, 7*s.* 6*d.*   1324.–1888.

BAND (fragment of) for a robe, of woven tapestry, coloured wools, and white flax. The pattern consists of repeated and balanced square forms. Amongst them is a green cross. From ancient tombs at Akhmîm (Panopolis), Upper Egypt. ? *Christian Coptic.* 4th to 7th centʸ. 8½ in. by 1½ in. Given by the Rev. Greville J. Chester.   1654.–1888.

BAND (part of, for a linen robe) of woven tapestry of dark blue wool in two stripes, edged with blue and red Greek crosses. From ancient tombs at Akhmîm (Panopolis), Upper Egypt. 4th to 7th centʸ. 9 in. by 3½ in. Given by the Rev. Greville J. Chester.   262.–1889.

BAND, (end of) for a linen robe, of woven tapestry, dark blue wool, and worked with needle in yellow flax thread. The pattern consists of repeated groups of two four-loop devices and a circular blossom shape, alternated with pointed oval spaces containing either a leaf, or scale device, &c., and bordered on each side with a narrow band of waved stem, leaf and fruit device. From ancient tombs at Akhmîm (Panopolis), Upper Egypt. ? 3rd to 9th centʸ. 2 ft. 4½ in. by 3½ in. Bought, 7*s.* 6*d.*   1323.–1888.

BAND, (portion of) for a linen robe, of woven tapestry, brown wool and yellow flax. The pattern consists of two intertwisted stems forming a series of oval spaces, the central one of which contains the bust of a man wearing a tunic with bands (*clavi*), and a small pendent ornament on his breast; in the other spaces are fruit (pomegranate) and floral (? tulip) devices, birds and hares. From ancient tombs at Akhm m (Panopolis), Upper Egypt. *Egypto-Roman.* ? 5th to 9th centʸ. 20 in. by 2 in. Bought (242 to 297, 29*l.* 9*s.* 6*d.*).

257.–1887.

BAND (portion of) for a linen robe, of woven tapestry, brown wool and yellow flax. The pattern consists of two intertwisted stems forming a series of oval spaces, the central one of which contains the bust of a man wearing a tunic with bands (*clavi*), and a small pendent ornament on his breast; in the other spaces are fruit (pomegranate) and floral (? tulip) devices, birds and hares. From ancient tombs at Akhmîm (Panopolis), Upper Egypt. *Egypto-Roman.* ? 5th to 9th centʸ. 20 in. by 2 in. Bought (242 to 297, 29*l.* 9*s.* 6*d.*).

257*a.*–1887.

BAND (part of) for a robe, of woven tapestry, yellow flax and dark purple wool. The pattern consists of a waved stem, between which are various running grotesque animals, lion, hare, dog, ? boar or pig, &c. Along each edge is a purple

band with semi-circular indents. From ancient tombs at
Akhmîm (Panopolis), Upper Egypt. *Egypto-Byzantine.* ? 5th
to 9th cent^y. About 15 in. by 2¾ in. Bought, 4s.

368.–1887.

BAND (portion of) for a linen robe, of woven tapestry, brown
wool and yellow flax. The pattern consists of two stems
intertwisted to form a series of oval spaces, within each of
which is a head, of a helmeted man, and man or woman with a
different sort of head-dress. From ancient tombs at Akhmîm
(Panopolis), Upper Egypt. *Egypto-Roman.* 5th to 9th cent^y.
L. 18 in. and 15 in. Bought 10s. the two.

1300, 1300a.–1888.

This specimen is made up of two fragments stitched together.

BAND (part of) for a linen robe, of woven tapestry, brown wool.
and yellow flax. The pattern consists of a continuous series
of diamond forms, within each of which, done in needlework,
is a border of guilloche device, and a small cross in the centre.
Beyond the diamond forms, at regular distances, are small
yellow blossoms; the edges of the band are of continuous
wave pattern. From ancient tombs at Akhmîm (Panopolis),
Upper Egypt. *Egypto-Roman.* 5th to 9th cent^y. 7 in. by
3 in. Bought, 5s. 306.–1889.

BANDS (triple for a linen robe), two, of diaper ornament, worked
with the needle in a short stitch with coloured wools and flax,
and central band of woven tapestry, coloured wool with
debased ornament. The two outer bands have little lozenge-
shaped pendants, the centre one has a pointed oval pendant.
From ancient tombs at Akhmîm (Panopolis), Upper Egypt.
? 6th to 9th cent^y. 20 in. by 10 in. Bought (242 to 297,
29l. 9s. 6d.). 258.–1887.

Tunics or robes with triple bands are worn at the present day by Arabs.

BANDS (triple, for a linen robe). The two outer ones are of
woven tapestry, coloured wool and white flax, with symmetrically planned ornament of debased leafy, animal and scroll devices. Each of these two bands has a pointed oval pendant, in
one of which is a face. The centre band is of embroidery in
short stitch, with coloured wool and white flax. The pendant
to this is a small diamond shape. From ancient tombs at
Akhmîm (Panopolis), Upper Egypt. ? 6th to 9th cent^y.
About 23 in. by 7 in. Bought (242 to 297, 29l. 9s. 6d.).

259.–1887.

Compare also with 258.–1887.

BAND (part of, for a linen robe) of woven tapestry, red and
blue wool, with a pattern of waved, fine, leafy stem winding
between triangles, and demi-ovals containing ornament.
From ancient tombs at Akhmîm (Panopolis), Upper Egypt.
? 6th to 9th cent^y. 12 in. by 2½ in. Bought (242 to 297,
29l. 9s. 6d.). 265.–1887.

The pattern here is on the same plan as that of 266.–1887.

BAND (part of, for a linen cloth) of woven tapestry, coloured wools (chiefly red) and white flax. The pattern consists of a series of small oblongs and quatrefoils placed about diamond spaces, within which are small roundels. From ancient tombs at Akhmim (Panopolis), Upper Egypt. ? 6th to 9th centy. 3 ft. 2 in. by 6 in. Bought (242 to 297, 29l. 9s. 6d.).

275.-1887.

BAND (fragment of) of woven tapestry in coloured wool and flax thread. The ornament consisted of two waved stems with leaf and semi-leaf shapes between them on a white ground. From ancient tombs at Akhmîm (Panopolis), Upper Egypt. ? 6th to 9th centy. 8 in. by 2¼ in. Bought (242 to 297, 29l. 9s. 6d.).

294.-1887.

BAND (portion of, from a linen robe), originally of woven tapestry, probably red wool and white flax, which last alone remains and indicates a pattern of repeated lozenge shapes, with borders of tree and reversed and counter-changed V devices From ancient tombs at Akhmîm (Panopolis), Upper Egypt ? 6th to 9th centy. 10⅝ in. by 4¾ in. Bought (994 to 1216 91l.).

1001.-1888.

BAND with round end and pendant (for a robe) of woven tapestry, coloured wools and yellow flax. The pattern probably was divided into three compartments, the upper one of which has been torn away. The upper of the two remaining compartments contains fragments of a figure group, of which one seems to be riding on some chimerical beast. At the back of this figure appears a smaller one bearing a flowering branch. The lower compartment contains a balanced arrangement of leaf and floral forms, a pair of cornucopiæ and birds, and a large central anthemion device. In the pendent panel are two seated figures, a male and female, one with a branch, one with a wreath(?). The band is edged with a black border, on which in colours are grotesque little birds, fishes, flowers, &c. From ancient tombs at Akhmîm (Panopolis), Upper Egypt. ? Egypto-Roman. 6th to 9th centy. 21 in. by 4 in. Bought, 1l. 15s.

1267.-1888.

Compare the pose of the figures in the pendent panel with that of the figures in roundel, No. 784.-1886.

BAND with round end and pendant (for a robe) of woven tapestry, coloured wools and yellow flax. The pattern (much degraded) consists of orderly and balanced groups of a quadruped, and (?)bird forms, a leaf device, and small round blossoms. Between these groups at the centre is a grotesque, richly-dressed figure (? the Virgin)* with nimbus. Her left hand is pointing upwards, and on her arm she seems to carry a ? flabellum. The pendent panel contains the figure of an animal. From ancient tombs at Akhmîm (Panopolis), Upper Egypt. Christian Coptic. ? 6th to 9th centy. 2 ft. 5 in. by 4 in. Bought, 1l. 10s.

1274.-1888.

* Compare with figure in No. 734.-1886.

BAND with round end (much eaten away) for a robe of woven tapestry, coloured wools and white flax thread. It is divided into three compartments. The central one contains the figure of a richly-robed saint with nimbus, the right hand pointing upwards, in the left a leaf branch or (?) *flabellum.* On the lower right hand corner are Greek characters (?) O Y C T. The lower compartment contains remains of grotesque human figures, animals and leaf devices in balanced arrangement. The upper compartment, from which all the wool has been eaten away, contained a similar arrangement of figures, &c. From ancient tombs at Akhmîm (Panopolis), Upper Egypt. *Christian Coptic.* ? 6th to 9th centy. 2 ft. by 4 in. Bought, 15s.   1297.–1888.

Compare also with No. 734.–1886 and 1274.–1888.

BAND (portion of) for a robe of woven tapestry, coloured wools and white flax (very fragmentary). Towards the centre is a degraded blossom form, on each side of which were grotesque animals (? dogs or gazelles). From ancient tombs at Akhmîm (Panopolis), Upper Egypt. *Christian Coptic.* ? 6th to 9th centy. 8½ in. by 4 in. Bought, 10s.   1304.–1888.

BANDS, stripes (fragments of), and detached blossom and other devices of woven tapestry, coloured wool inwoven into linen for a tunic. From ancient tombs at Akhmîm (Panopolis), Upper Egypt. ? 6th to 9th centy. 14 in. by 5 in. Bought, 7s. 6d.   1319.–1888.

See note to 1363.–1888.

BAND (fragment of) with two narrow bands of continuous waved stem and leaf ornament, between which are large red leaf and other detached forms of woven tapestry, coloured wools inwoven into linen. From ancient tombs at Akhmîm (Panopolis), Upper Egypt. ? 6th to 9th centy. 12 in. by 2¼ in. Bought, 6s.   1341.–1888.

See note to **1363.–1888.**

BAND (fragment of) with repeated double vertical series of rude leaf and blossom forms of woven tapestry, coloured wools inwoven into linen. From ancient tombs at Akhmîm (Panopolis), Upper Egypt. ? 6th to 9th centy. 12 in. by 2 in. Bought, 5s.   1360.–1888.

See note to 1363.–1888.

BAND (fragment of) for a robe, of woven tapestry, coloured wool. The ornament consists of a grotesque lion, a harpy,(?) a roundel in which is a head with large ornaments, and part of dog.(?) From ancient tombs at Akhmîm (Panopolis), Upper Egypt. ? *Christian Coptic.* ? 6th to 9th centy. About 14 in. by 5 in. Given by the Rev. Greville J. Chester.   1663.–1888.

14

BAND (fragment of) for a linen robe of woven tapestry and
needlework, brown wool and yellow flax thread. From
ancient tombs at Akhmîm (Panopolis), Upper Egypt. ? 6th
to 9th cent⁷. 5 in. by 3 in. Given by the Rev. Greville J.
Chester. 1664.-1888.

BAND (part of) for a robe, of woven tapestry, coloured wool,
with degraded ornament composed of figures within two
ovals: between the ovals are representations of the cross
supported by wings, suggestive of the ancient Egyptian
winged discs. From ancient tombs at Akhmîm (Panopolis),
Upper Egypt. *Christian Coptic.* 6th to 9th cent⁷. 8 in.
by 4 in. Given by the Rev. Greville J. Chester. 256.-1889.

BAND (part of) for a robe, of woven tapestry, coloured wools,
with pattern of repeated diamonds and half hexagons. From
ancient tombs at Akhmîm (Panopolis), Upper Egypt. ? 6th
to 9th cent⁷. 10 in. by 3½ in. Given by the Rev. Greville
J. Chester. 263.-1889.

BAND (fragment of) for a robe, of woven tapestry, coloured
wools. The lower square of the band is set with a yellow
roundel, containing a debased figure of a green bird. From
ancient tombs at Akhmîm (Panopolis), Upper Egypt. ? 6th
to 9th cent⁷. 3½ in. by 1¾ in. Given by the Rev. Greville
J. Chester. 265.-1889.

BAND (portion of, ? for a robe) of woven tapestry, coloured
wools, with alternating stripes of dark blue, with outline
guilloche pattern worked with the needle, and of yellow with
a series of red heart shapes. From ancient tombs at Akhmîm
(Panopolis), Upper Egypt. ? 6th to 9th cent⁷. 18½ in. by
6¼ in. Bought, 1l. 5s. 278.-1889.

BANDS (portion of two shoulder), with pointed ends and pendent
stems of woven tapestry, coloured wools. The ornament consists of repeated stems, with flower and fruit ornament of
degraded form. From ancient tombs at Akhmîm (Panopolis),
Upper Egypt. ? 6th to 9th cent⁷. 13 in. by 5½ in. Bought,
10s. 290.-1889.

BAND (part of), round ended, with a stem and pendent panel
of woven tapestry, purple and black wool. The edges of the
band and the lower stem are of spotted purple ornament on
black; the inner ground of the band is purple, with rude
blossom and leafy stem devices in black. From ancient tombs
at Akhmîm (Panopolis), Upper Egypt. ? 6th to 9th cent⁷.
16 in. by 4 in. Bought, 6s. 297.-1889.

BAND (portion of) for a robe, of tapestry, woven with brown
wool and yellow flax. The pattern consists of a series of
roundels or circular panels, within which are fruit, leaf, bird,
and other devices. Along each edge of the band is a waved
stem with blossom and leaf ornament. From ancient tombs
at Akhmîm (Panopolis), Upper Egypt. ? *Egypto-Byzantine.*
6th to 9th cent⁷. 2 ft. 2 in. by 7½ in. Bought, 6s.
298.-1889.

BAND (portion of) for a linen robe, of woven tapestry and needlework, brown wool and white flax. The pattern consists of repeated long stem and scroll devices. ? 6th to 9th cent?. L. 14 in., W. 1 in. Given by the Greville J. Chester.
219.–1890.

BAND of ornament worked in the manner of tapestry weaving, with a repeating pattern of star and intertwisting devices alternated, in blue and red silks. From ancient tombs at Akhmim (Panopolis), Upper Egypt. ? Saracenic. 7th to 11th cent?. 7½ in. by 5 in. Bought, 5s. 1357.–1888.

BAND (fragment of) of woven tapestry, red and yellow silks on fine flax warp. This fragment is of a double border, the central portion of which has a sort of trellis pattern of intertwisting narrow bands, between which are debased renderings of birds, animals, and tree forms repeated : beyond on each are sham Kufic inscriptions in red. From ancient tombs at Erment, Upper Egypt. Saracenic. 7th to 11th cent?. 10 in. by 7 in. Bought, 4s. 1382.–1888.
See smaller similar fragment No. 305.–1890.

BAND (fragment of) of woven tapestry, faded red, yellow, and black silks on fine flax warps. This is a double band. The central portion of each band contains a succession of small black outlined roundels : beyond, on each side, are indistinct imitation Kufic characters in red, and beyond again (on the upper band) on each side are smaller imitation Kufic characters in black. From ancient tombs at Akhmim (Panopolis), Upper Egypt. Saracenic. ? 7th to 11th cent?. About 13 in. by 9 in. Given by the Rev. Greville J. Chester. 1661.–1888.
See also 327.–1889. Both these specimens are of somewhat similar work to the lower narrow border of 8827.–1863, p. 113 of Catalogue.

BAND (fragment of) of woven tapestry, faded red, yellow, and black silks on fine flax warps. The central portion contains a succession of small black outlined roundels ; on each side of it in red are indistinct imitation Kufic inscriptions, and beyond on each side in black are smaller inscriptions. From ancient tombs at Akhmim (Panopolis), Upper Egypt. Saracenic. ? 7th to 11th cent?. 13¼ in. by 6¼ in. Given by the Rev. Greville J. Chester. 327.-1889.
See also 1661.–1888.

BAND (fragment of) of woven tapestry, yellow and red silk on fine flax warps. The pattern on the main portion consisted of intertwisting narrow bands, between which are debased renderings of birds and ? tree forms ; on the upper side is a sham Kufic inscription in red. Saracenic. 7th to 11th cent?. 6⅝ in. by 4 in. Given by the Rev. Greville J. Chester.
305.–1890.
See also 1382.–1888 of similar work.

(d.) COLLAR; CUFF (bands for).

COLLAR (for a robe) of woven tapestry, brown wool and yellow flax thread. The pattern consists of repeated anthemion or honeysuckle ornaments set between plain brown bands; near the neck are little white square dots. From ancient tombs at Akhmîm (Panopolis), Upper Egypt. ? *Egypto-Greek.* ? 1st centy. B.C. 13 in. by 2¼ in. Bought, 15s. 1296.-1888.

This is unlike any specimen hitherto taken from Akhmim. The shape of the neck trimming is specially noticeable, as it seems to have come from a robe cut on a different pattern from that of the Roman tunics or later date. The character of the honeysuckles is of a Greek rather than a Roman type.

CUFF (two narrow bands for) of woven tapestry and needlework, red wool and yellow flax on small warp threads, from a linen robe. The pattern in each band is the same, and consists of a horizontal arrangement of small animal forms, ? a goat and a lion alternated, with tiny fish and serpents near their heads : in between them are two little kneeling human figures bearing ? vases. At the ends of each band are leaf and bird devices, and on each is a continuous wave ornament. From ancient tombs at Akhmîm (Panopolis). Upper Egypt. *Egypto-Roman.* 1st to 6th centy. 10 in. by 5½ in. Bought, 1l. 5s.

1281.-1888.

Compare this with No. 1292.-1888. **The style of** the design is Roman. The weaving is noticeable for its fine warps.

CUFF (two narrow bands for) of woven tapestry and needlework, red wool and yellow flax on small warp threads, from a linen robe. The pattern in each band is the same, and consists of a vertical arrangement (as in pilasters) of a vase or basket (*calathus*), a group of balanced scroll ornament, a straight stem with a snake twisted along, and around it (? *caduceus*) a small group of ? vase forms, from which sprout two stems enclosing a bird. From ancient tombs at Akhmîm (Panopolis), Upper Egypt. *Egypto-Roman,* ? 1st to 6th centy. 11 in. by 6 in. Bought, 1l. 1292.-1888.

Compare this with No. 1281.-1888. The style of the ornament is Roman. The weaving is noticeable for its fine warp.

CUFF (two broad bands for) of woven tapestry, brown and occasional red wools, and yellow flax. The pattern consists of an acanthus scroll enclosing a series of spaces, in each of which is an animal, such as a hare, dog, lion, ibex. From ancient tombs at Akhmîm (Panopolis), Upper Egypt. *Egypto-Roman.* 3rd to 6th centy. 13½ in. by 6¾ in. Bought (242 to 297, 29l. 9s. 6d.). 253.-1887.

See also acanthus scroll in No. 348.-1890.

CUFF (two bands for) of woven tapestry, brown wool and yellow flax. The pattern consists of a triple leaf, long stem spray, and an elongated animal (? ibex), repeated and interchanged. From ancient tombs at Akhmîm (Panopolis), Upper Egypt. *Egypto-Roman.* 3rd to 6th centy. 10½ in. by 3½ in. Bought (242 to 297, 29l. 9s. 6d.). 255.-1887.

CUFF (two bands for) of woven tapestry, coloured wool. The pattern consists of a series of small heart or petal-shape forms,* alternately blue and red, on a brown ground, the outer edges of which are of the continuous wave device. From ancient tombs at Akhmîm (Panopolis), Upper Egypt. *Egypto-Roman.* 3rd to 6th centʸ. 11 in. by 5½ in. Bought, 6s. 1339.-1888.

* See similar devices in frame of No. 654.-1886.

CUFF (part of band for a) of woven tapestry and needlework, brown wool and yellow flax. The pattern consists of a vertical series of vase shapes with two floriated branches in each. From ancient tombs at Akhmîm (Panopolis), Upper Egypt. ? *Egypto-Roman.* 3rd to 6th centʸ. 7 in. by 3 in. Bought, 5s. 1347.-1888.

CUFF (pair of narrow bands for a) of woven tapestry, coloured wool. The pattern consists of repeated small tree devices. From ancient tombs at Akhmîm (Panopolis), Upper Egypt. ? 3rd to 6th centʸ. About 10 in. by 3 in. Bought, 5s. 1352.-1888.

CUFF BAND (fragment of ?) of woven tapestry, dark blue wool and yellow flax. The pattern consists of a waved stem with short scrolls and vine leaves. From ancient tombs at Akhmîm (Panopolis), Upper Egypt. ? *Egypto-Roman.* 3rd to 6th centʸ. 8½ in. by ¾ in. Bought, 3s. 1374.-1888.

CUFF (part of band for a) of woven tapestry, brown, yellow, and red wools. With a pattern of circles containing ? black triskeles on red roundels; at each end of the band is a rude rendering of a bird in black on yellow. From ancient tombs at Akhmîm (Panopolis), Upper Egypt. ? 3rd to 6th centʸ. 11 in. by 1¼ in. Bought, 2s. 6d. 1375.-1888.

CUFF (part of, from a linen robe) with a band of woven tapestry, coloured wools. The ornament consists of a central stripe of zigzag line and spots, flanked by a waved stem, and bud and flower ornament. From an ancient Roman cemetery in the Fayûm, Middle Egypt. ? 3rd to 9th centʸ. 8 in. by 5½ in. Given by H. M. Kennard, Esq. 321.-1889.

CUFF (two bands for) of woven tapestry, brown wool and yellow flax. The pattern on each band consists of two intertwisted stems forming a series of oval spaces in each of which is either a fruit or floral spray or hare or bird. From ancient tombs at Akhmîm (Panopolis), Upper Egypt. *Egypto-Roman.* 5th to 9th centʸ. 11 in. by 4½ in. Bought (242 to 297, 29l. 9s. 6d.). 256.-1887.

This ornament evidently belonged to the robe for which the bands 257 and 257a.-1887 belonged.

CUFF (part of) of linen, with a band of woven tapestry, coloured wools. The pattern consists of semi-circular forms interchanged at regular distances with semi-quatrefoil forms, within each of which are small fruit and basket devices, &c.; between these forms are obliquely set small scrolls. A narrow band of black and red wools woven with two ornaments, alternated and repeated, is stitched on. From an ancient tomb in Egypt. *Egypto-Byzantine.* Probably 7th to 9th cent⸱. About 10 in. by 9 in. Given by Mrs. Goodison.

348.–1887.

(e.) SQUARE PANELS (*tabulæ*) for shoulders and skirts of robes, chiefly of the tunic class.

SQUARE PANEL (part of only) of woven tapestry, coloured wools and white flax. This is one side of a border to a square panel for a cover or cloth (see Mat, 655.–1886). The ornament consists of four circular panels enclosed by scrolls with rude fruit and floral devices, within which are purple animals picked out with white and yellow spots and red tongues. From ancient tombs at Akhmîm (Panopolis), Upper Egypt. ?*Egypto-Roman.* 1st to 4th cent⸱. 12 in. by 3¼ in. Bought, 1*l.*

1288.–1888.

SQUARE PANEL of woven tapestry, brown wool and yellow flax; part of a linen robe. In the central medallion is a radiating device of four vases with trefoil stems; beyond, one at each corner, are four mounted huntsmen in confronting pairs, each huntsman holding ? a wreath; between them are various animals, ? ibex, lion, and dog. From ancient tombs at Akhmîm (Panopolis), Upper Egypt. *Egypto-Roman.* ? 1st to 5th cent⸱. 6 in. square. Bought (242 to 297, 29*l.* 9*s.* 6*d.*). 244.–1887.

SQUARE PANEL of woven tapestry, dark-brown wool and yellow flax; part of a linen robe. In the central oval is a nude male figure holding a hook or ? sickle; around is a border of two intertwisted stems forming a series of circular panels, in each of which, alternately, is a blossom and a leaf. Part of the band or *clavus* of similar pattern as the border is with the square. The border and square are edged with continuous pattern of wave device. From ancient tombs at Akhmîm (Panopolis), Upper Egypt. *Egypto-Roman.* ? 1st to 5th cent⸱. Bought.

411.–1887.

SQUARE PANEL of woven tapestry and needlework, brown wool and yellow flax. The border consists of a blossom at each corner and a double reversed leaf device between them. In a central roundel is a representation of the toilet of Venus; the goddess appears to be holding up the ends of her hair; beside her are a hand-mirror or *patella*, and an unguent box or *cista.* At each corner beyond the centre roundel is a fish.

From ancient tombs at Akhmîm (Panopolis), Upper Egypt. *Egypto-Roman.* 1st to 5th centy. 7½ in. by 6 in. Bought, 1*l.* 5*s.* 1280.–1888.

See also the *cista* in No. 273.–1889.

SQUARE PANEL of woven tapestry, red wool and yellow flax; part of a child's tunic. The pattern consists of a wave-patterned square border, within which is a circle containing in even distribution a central figure playing a harp (? Apollo or Orpheus), about him are various human figures, animals, &c., a boy with a duck, a winged figure with a cornucopia, an ass, a lion, &c. In the four corners beyond the circle are debased animal and bird forms. From ancient tombs at Akhmîm (Panopolis), Upper Egypt. *Egypto-Roman.* ? 1st to 5th centy. 8 in. by 3 in. Bought, 1*l.* 1290.–1888.

This piece is remarkable for the minuteness of the work. The action of the man playing the harp is well rendered.

TUNIC, part of skirt, of rough towel material, faced with flax loops, with a square panel of woven tapestry, originally of red and green wools and yellow flax; much of the wool eaten away. The pattern consisted of a head set in a yellow cir-cular medallion, within a green square, surrounded by a red and yellow border of repeated diamond and small square devices edged on outer side with continuous wave pattern ornament in green. From ancient tombs at Akhmîm (Pano-polis), Upper Egypt. *Egypto-Roman.* ? 1st to 5th centy. 9 in. square. Bought, 10*s.* 1307.–1888.

Compare head with that in 272.–1889.

SQUARE PANEL of woven tapestry in variously coloured wools for a robe. Within a frame of red and yellow bands, on a black ground, is the head of a youth wearing a green tunic with narrow bands (*clavi*) and shoulder roundels (*orbiculi*). From ancient tombs at Akhmîm (Panopolis), Upper Egypt. *Egypto-Roman.* ? 1st to 5th centy. 8¼ in. by 8 in. Bought, 3*l.* 269.–1889.

This panel may have been intended for a curtain, hanging, or cover. Ptolemy Philadelphus is reputed to have had in his dining hall splendid hangings depicting the portraits of kings or the stories of mythology. The style of the portrait is similar to that of the painted panel portraits found in the Fayûm, of which a specimen, No. 1695.–1888, is in the S.K. Museum.

SQUARE PANEL of woven tapestry in variously coloured wools for a robe.* Within a frame of red and yellow bands on a black ground is the head of a woman wearing a jewelled diadem* or fillet. About her head is a green medallion (? a nimbus) ; she wears ear-rings and a circular pendant on her breast (? a *bulla aurea*). From ancient tombs at Akhmîm (Panopolis), Upper Egypt. *Egypto-Roman.* ? 1st to 5th centy. 8¼ in. square. Bought, 3*l.* 270.–1889.

* See similar diadem worn by the angel figure in specimen No. 349.–1887, as well as examples of cut leather fillets (found in the Fayûm and elsewhere in Egypt), Nos. 372.–1887 and 8.–1888 in the S.K. Museum. This panel seems to have been one of a set with No. 269.–1889.

SQUARE PANEL of woven tapestry, red wool, and yellow flax;
part of a child's linen tunic or robe. In a central oval medallion is a rudely drawn human head in brown wool and yellow
flax ; a continuous wave pattern runs round the square, and
on each side of small bit of shoulder band (or *clavus*) which is
attached to the linen on which the square is fastened. From
ancient tomos at Akhmîm (Panopolis), Upper Egypt. *? Egypto-
Roman.* ? 1st to 5th cent^y. 3¼ in. by 2 in. Bought, 1*l*.

272.–1889.

SQUARE PANEL (for a linen tunic) of woven tapestry, purple and
coloured wool and yellow flax. In a central white roundel is
a nude armed figure with a coloured scarf and a shield on his
left arm. The border consists of repeated white circles containing a cross device on purple ground. From ancient
tombs at Akhmîm (Panopolis), Upper Egypt. *? Egypto-Roman.*
? 1st to 6th cent^y. 11 in. by 10¼ in. Bought (994 to 1216,
91*l*.). 997.–1888.

SQUARE PANEL (? for a tunic) of woven tapestry, chiefly purple
wool and white flax. On a white ground is a red-legged
partridge; to the right a small leafy bush, and below on the
left a smaller three-leafed branch. A guilloche pattern in
needlework runs along the square border. From ancient
tombs at Akhmîni (Panopolis), Upper Egypt. *Egypto-Roman.*
? 1st to 6th cent^y. 10½ in. by 8½ in. Bought, 2*l*.

1265.–1888.

SQUARE PANEL, for a tunic, of woven tapestry, purple and
yellow wool, delicately worked over with the needle in fine
yellow and white-flax threads. The pattern consists of a yellow
medallion in the centre bearing a four-leafed cross device, and
set within an eight-pointed star panel, the ground of which is
filled in with intertwisted bands forming a series of linked
roundels; beyond this the ground is filled with an angular
stem and leaf pattern, which is enclosed by a square border
of guilloche ornament; the whole is bounded by a purple-
edged square border of linked roundels (purple on a yellow
ground), picked out with small rope ornament, and a leaf
within each roundel. From ancient tombs at Akhmîm (Panopolis), Upper Egypt. *Egypto-Roman.* ? 1st to 6th cent^y.
12 in. square. Bought, 1*l*. 10s. 1276.–1888.

For delicate tracery of ornament this specimen is noticeable. On an even smaller
scale is the work on a little square panel, No. 1310.–1888.

SQUARE PANEL (for a linen robe) of woven tapestry, fine
coloured wools. In the centre with a white ground is a
roundel containing a red-legged and beaked blue bird with
leafy sprays ; this roundel is set in a brown square, which is
bordered with small brown roundels containing blossoms,
between which are leaf and bud devices on a yellow ground

edged with brown. From ancient tombs at Akhmîm (Panopolis), Upper Egypt. *Egypto-Roman.* ? 1st to 6th centy. 6 in. square. Bought, 1*l.* 1285.-1888.

This specimen is of as fine a texture as the specimens Nos. 651.-1886, 652.-1886, &c.

SQUARE PANEL (for a tunic) of woven tapestry, purple wool, and yellow flax with needle-work in yellow wool. The centre contains a purple floriated cross device on a yellow ground, surrounded by a square border of delicately worked guilloche device; and an outer border (edged with tassel and trefoil devices) similarly worked with a double scrolled band forming diamond spaces, within which are outlined blossoms. From ancient tombs at Akhmîm (Panopolis), Upper Egypt. *Egypto-Roman.* ? 1st to 6th centy. 11½ in. by 10½ in. Bought, 1*l.* 1289.-1888

SQUARE PANEL (for a child's tunic) of woven tapestry, brown wool delicately worked over with the needle in fine flax threads. The device in the centre consists of two interlaced oval bands, with a plain brown square border to them, which is enclosed by a small guilloche device border, edged with points, and a trefoil at each corner. From ancient tombs at Akhmîm (Panopolis), Upper Egypt. *Egypto-Roman.* ? 1st to 6th centy. The linen is 6 in. by 4 in.; the panel is 1½ in. square. Bought, 10*s.* 1310.-1888.

This is the smallest and daintiest specimen of this class of work in the S.K. Museum.

SQUARE PANEL of woven tapestry and needlework, brown wool and yellow flax; part of a linen robe. The border consists of a double stem intertwined to form a series of circular spaces, within each of which is a blossom; in the centre of the piece is a lion. From ancient tombs at Akhmîm (Panopolis), Upper Egypt. ? 1st to 6th centy. 4 in. by 3½ in. Bought, 10*s.* 1311.-1888.

Compare the lion with those in tunic No. 631.-1886, pp. 17 and 18 of catalogue. The treatment of the mane is similar to that adopted in Greek work on a metal bowl found at Cyprus of the 5th or 6th century B.C.

SQUARE PANEL (for a tunic) of fine woven tapestry, dark purple wool and flax thread. The inner ground is covered with a check or chess-board pattern, and is surrounded by a border divided into four equal rectangular panellings containing a pattern of crosses (*pattées*) within diamonds. From ancient tombs at Akhmîm (Panopolis), Upper Egypt. *Egypto-Roman.* ? 1st to 6th centy. 5 in. by 4½ in. Bought, 6*s.* 295.-1889.

SQUARE PANEL (fragmentary), for a tunic, of woven tapestry, purple wool, worked over in white and yellow threads with the needle. The pattern consists of a leaf in the centre, set in an eight-pointed star, the ground of which is filled in with a sort of guilloche ornament. The star is set within double square borders, the inner one of which has a different version of the guilloche device; the outer one having an intertwisted stem forming a series of circular spaces, in each of which is leaf form. From ancient tombs at Akhmîm (Panopolis), Upper Egypt. *Egypto-Roman.* ? 1st to 6th cent⁷. 8 in. square. Bought, 6s. 299.–1889.

SQUARE PANEL (corner fragment of) of woven tapestry, coloured wools, with a figure of a running warrior carrying a short sword and shield set on a white ground, within a roundel surrounded by purple. From ancient tombs at Akhmîm (Panopolis), Upper Egypt. *Egypto-Roman.* ? 1st to 6th cent⁷ 4 in. by 4¾ in. Given by the Rev. Greville J. Chester.
353.–1890.
See similar figures in more complete squares, such as Nos. 711.–1886; 712.–1886.

SQUARE PANEL (small), for a linen robe, of woven tapestry, blue wool and white flax, with a four-arm, triple-branched device, between which appears a smaller leaf-ended, equal-limb cross. From ancient tombs at Akhmîm (Panopolis), Upper Egypt. *Egypto-Roman.* ? 2nd to 6th cent⁷. 3 in. square. Bought (242 to 297, 29l. 9s. 6d.). 249.–1887.

SQUARE PANEL of woven tapestry, brown wool and white flax, part of a linen robe. The pattern consists of an orderly arrangement of nine medallions, within each of eight of which is a floriated (?) anchor device; the central medallion contains an animal form. From ancient tombs at Akhmîm (Panopolis), Upper Egypt. *Egypto-Roman.* ? 2nd to 6th cent⁷. 7 in. square. Bought, 1l. 5s. 1282.–1888.

SQUARE PANEL (small), for a linen robe, of woven tapestry, brown wool and yellow flax thread, with two oval-shape bands interlaced in the centre, and small medallions containing masks or heads at the corners. From ancient tombs at Akhmîm (Panopolis), Upper Egypt. *Egypto-Roman.* ? 2nd to 6th cent⁷. 3¼ in. by 2¾ in. Bought, 7s. 6d. 1315.–1888.

SQUARE PANEL of woven tapestry, brown wool and yellow flax, part of a linen robe or tunic. In the roundel is a degraded representation of a hunter on horseback with his dog. This is enclosed within a square border, each corner being filled in with leaf and scroll device. From ancient tombs at Akhmîm (Panopolis), Upper Egypt. ? 2nd to 6th cent⁷. With the fragments of linen garment, about 4 in. square. Bought, 1l.
256.–1890.

OBLONG PANEL of woven tapestry, coloured wools; for a linen robe. The design consists of *tau* cross and circular disc, (*crux ansata*) jewelled, within the loop or disc is a human face wearing a cap; below the arms of the cross are two amphora shaped vases, with two foliated branches in each; above the disc are two similar vases, between which is a small foliated cross device. About this evenly balanced group is a rectangular border, beyond which is a border of waved

stem and ivy-leaf device. From ancient tombs at Akhmim (Panopolis), Upper Egypt. *Egypto-Roman.* ? 3rd to 5th centy. 9 in. by 6¼ in. Bought, 1*l.* 259.-1890.
See also 258.-1890.

SQUARE PANEL (fragment of), for a linen robe, of woven tapestry, brown, red, yellow, and green wools, and yellow flax. The pattern consists of a central degraded group, (?) human figure on horseback in brown on a yellow ground, encircled by a band with red wave ornament, set within a square, at the corners of which are (?) leaves. Beyond the surrounding border is made up of white blossom forms and red (?) fruit forms, alternated. From ancient tombs at Akhmim (Panopolis), Upper Egypt. *Egypto-Roman.* 3rd to 6th centy. About 6 in. square. Bought, 7*s.* 1334.-1888.

SQUARE PANEL (for a linen tunic) of woven tapestry, coloured wool and yellow flax. The pattern consists of a small, dark, circular band, enclosing four alternately red and green trefoils; this is set within a dark square band, beyond which, and forming the outer square border, are red circular devices with dots in them at the corners, and between them rude, serrated ornament and diamond shapes. From ancient tombs at Akhmim (Panopolis), Upper Egypt. ? 3rd to 6th centy. About 10 in. square. Bought (242 to 297, 29*l.* 9*s.* 6*d.*). 248.-1887.

SQUARE PANEL (for a child's linen robe) of woven tapestry, purple worsted and white flax. The pattern consists of a small central disc, towards which, from the corners of the square, converge four triple-branched, formal leaf devices. From ancient tombs at Akhmim (Panopolis), Upper Egypt. ? 3rd to 6th centy. About 3 in. square. Bought (242 to 297, 29*l.* 9*s.* 6*d.*). 250.-1887.

SQUARE PANEL (for a linen robe or tunic) of woven tapestry and needlework, dark blue wool and yellow flax. On a yellow ground in the centre of the square is a vase with balanced leafy stems within a circular band. The square band beyond has a border of guilloche ornament in outline. From ancient tombs at Akhmim (Panopolis), Upper Egypt. ? *Egypto-Roman.* ? 3rd to 6th centy. 4 in. square. Bought (242 to 297, 29*l.* 9*s.* 6*d.*). 251.-1887.

SQUARE PANEL (from a child's linen tunic) of woven tapestry (very fine warp and weft threads), coloured silk. In the centre is a circle containing the figure of a horseman mounted on a white horse; in the spandrils at the inner corners of the enclosing square band are small scroll devices, and in the border are fruits, ducks, and fishes. The ground throughout is green. From ancient tombs in Egypt. ? *Egypto-Roman.* 3rd to 6th centy. About 4 in. square. Bought, 5*l.* 334.-1887.

This and No. 335.-1887 (band) from the same robe are of very delicate texture and minute work.

SQUARE PANEL (for a linen tunic) of woven tapestry, purple
wool and yellow flax, with a bird in each of the four corners,
separated by vases containing vines; in the centre is a series
of three crosses laid on one another in whitish thread on a
purple ground; the devices are divided from one another
by an intertwining purple band. From ancient tombs at
Akhmîm (Panopolis), Upper Egypt. ? *Egypto-Roman.* 3rd
to 6th centy. 4⅔ in. by 4⅔ in. Given by the Rev. Greville
J. Chester. 355.-1890.

See also 356.-1890.

SQUARE PANEL (for a linen tunic) of woven tapestry, purple
wool and white flax, with a wild animal in each of the corners,
separated by vases containing vines; in the centre is a conventional floral pattern; the devices are divided from one
another by an intertwining purple band. From ancient
tombs at Akhmîm (Panopolis), Upper Egypt. *Egypto-Roman.* ?
3rd to 6th centy. 7 in. by 6 in. Given by the Rev. Greville
J. Chester. 356.-1890.

See also 355.-1890.

SQUARE PANEL (from a woollen robe or cloth), of woven tapestry,
coloured wools, and needlework of white flax in parts. The
pattern consists of an arrangement of oblongs and squares
bordered by light green bands decorated with a pattern in
whitish flax filled in alternately with groups of debased forms
of animals and of two forms ? a lion and a fish, within yellow
circular bands and blossoms at the corners. *Egypto-Roman.*
3rd to 6th centy. 11½ in. by 10¼ in. Bought, 2l.

643.-1890.

The style of this specimen resembles that of a panel found at Thebes by Mr. Hay
and now in the British Museum, and mentioned p. 142, chap. IX., in Sir G. Wilkinson's
Ancient Egyptians.

OBLONG PANEL, made up of two fragments (for a cloak ?*), of
woven tapestry and needlework, the border of coloured wools,
the main ground of brown wool worked in flax outline with
an intercrossing circle and other diaper pattern, filled in with
various sized circles and diamonds. From ancient tombs at
Akhmîm (Panopolis), Upper Egypt. *Egypto-Roman.* 4th to
6th centy. 20 in. by 17 in.. Bought, 10s. the two.

1298, 1298a.-1888.

* See use of this sort of large panel on the cloak of an attendant standing on the
right hand of the Empress Theodora in the Ravenna Mosaic (6th century); also on
the cloak of Emperor Arcadius in a silver dish (4th century) found at Estremadura.

SQUARE PANEL of woven tapestry, brown wool and yellow flax,
stitched to a bit of a linen robe. The central device is a
floriated cross, the outer border to it is of repeated scrolling
stems with an ornamental leaf. From ancient tombs at
Akhmîm (Panopolis), Upper Egypt. ? 4th to 6th centy. 3½ in.
square. Bought, 6s. 1338.-1888.

SQUARE PANEL (fragmentary), from a linen tunic, of woven
tapestry and needlework, fine red-brown wool and brown flax
on small flax warps. The square originally contained a representation of two mounted hunters chasing ? a lion and ? a
leopard or panther. The border consists of intertwisted stems
or narrow bands forming a series of circles enclosing either a
lotus flower, or a cruciform, or a duck. From ancient tombs
at Hawara, Middle Egypt. 4th or 5th centy. H. 8½ in.,
W. 6½ in. Bought, 1*l.* 10*s*. 439.–1889.

The make of this specimen from Hawara, in Middle Egypt, resembles that of the
pieces from Upper and Lower Egypt, thereby pointing to a common practice of
this weaving throughout Egypt at this period.

SQUARE PANEL (for a tunic) of woven tapestry, dark blue wool
and discoloured flax thread. The pattern consists of a small
inner roundel, enclosing crossed leafy stems; this roundel with
four outer plain leafy stems is set within an eight-pointed star
panel, with crossed leafy stems between the points, and this
again is bounded by a square border of waved stem, grape
and vine leaf devices. From ancient tombs at Akhmîm
(Panopolis), Upper Egypt. ? 4th to 6th centy. 5½ in. square.
Bought, 5*s*. 1350.–1888.

SQUARE PANEL (the wool entirely eaten away) for a linen robe,
originally of woven tapestry. The pattern consisting of two
pairs of animals *vis-à-vis*, balanced floral stems, and small
ornamental devices at the corners, is indicated by the flax
threads only From ancient tombs at Akhmîm (Panopolis),
Upper Egypt. ? 3rd to 7th centy. 6½ in. by 4¾ in. Bought,
(242 to 297, 29*l*. 9*s*. 6*d*.). 271.–1887

The specimen is interesting as showing the flax threads, which may have been
the first to be worked into the warp; the coloured wools would then have been worked
in after the pattern had been completely indicated with the flax threads.

SQUARE PANEL (fragmentary) of woven tapestry and needlework, purple wool and yellow flax; for a linen robe. The
ground in the centre is covered with a diaper key pattern, in
some of the squares of which, at regular intervals, are small
yellow quatrefoil blossoms, and wreaths (in outline); the border
is of waved stem and leaf ornament. From ancient tombs at
Akhmîm (Panopolis), Upper Egypt. ? 3rd to 9th centy. About
10 in. by 8 in. Bought, 7*s*. 6*d*. 1317.–1888.

SQUARE PANEL of woven tapestry, brown wool and yellow flax;
part of a linen robe. In the centre is a circular panel containing a close and orderly arrangement of ? debased animal
and floral forms. From ancient tombs at Akhmîm (Panopolis),
Upper Egypt. ? 3rd to 9th centy. 3 in. square. Bought, 10*s*.
287.–1889.

SQUARE PANELS (a pair, fragmentary) of woven tapestry, red
wool and yellow flax, on small warp threads; for a child's
tunic. The ornament in each panel consists of a white
circular band, with alternate crescents and leafy stems in red,

enclosing a group of two horses, back to back, with heads turned, and a balanced ornamental device between them, and a second at their hoofs. From ancient tombs at Akhmîm (Panopolis), Upper Egypt. ? *Egypto-Roman.* ? 5th to 9th cent. About 6 in. by 5 in. Bought (242 to 297, 29*l.* 9*s.* 6*d.*).

279.–1887.

See Anastasius Bibliothecarius (9th cent') on use of such patterns in woven fabrics ; also Sidonius Apollinaris (5th cent'). These may possibly date from earlier than the 5th cent. For fineness of weaving they compare with Nos. 1292 and 1281.—1888.

SQUARE PANEL of woven tapestry, chiefly brown and white wool. The border to the square consists of repeated similar devices; within this is a circular intercrossing double band ornament, within which is a man riding a grotesque beast or chimera with open mouth. The man appears to have just shot a shaft ? from his small bow. From ancient tombs at Akhmîm (Panopolis), Upper Egypt. ?7th cent. 7 in. by 6 in. Bought, 1*l.* 10*s.*
1275.–1888.

PORTION OF A GARMENT? of linen, originally ornamented with stripes and sprigs of woven tapestry, coloured wools. Applied to it are fragments of two square panels of coloured silk weaving. The pattern on these consisted of circular bands of floral devices enclosing two horsemen confronted, and each spearing a wild beast, with a pair of dogs below the beasts. From ancient tombs at Akhmîm (Panopolis), Upper Egypt. ? *Syrian.* ? 6th to 9th cent. Greatest H. 17½ in., W. 2 ft. 0½ in. Bought (with 108 and 109), 25*l.*
107.–1887.

The group of the hunters on horseback, with hounds, &c. as here originally pour-trayed was a favourite subject with Eastern weavers in the 5th and later centuries. It is mentioned by Sidonius Apollinaris. (5th cent'.) See similar group, as here figured, in tapestry woven medallion, No. 862.–1836.
The tapestry woven ornament appears to belong to the class of work referred to in note to 1363.–1888, of the 6th to 9th centuries.

SQUARE PANEL (for a linen robe) of woven tapestry, red, blue, and black wool. The pattern consists of a leafy trellis with lozenge and circular devices alternating in the enclosed spaces. From ancient tombs at Akhmîm (Panopolis), Upper Egypt. ? 6th to 9th cent. About 8½ in. square. Bought (242 to 297, 29*l.* 9*s.* 6*d.*).
266.–1887.

See also 896.–1886 and 282.–1889.

SQUARE PANEL (for a linen tunic) of woven tapestry, coloured wool and yellow flax. The pattern, on a red ground, consists of a trellis with white bars ornamented with repeated green S devices terminated with red leaves ; in the diamond shapes are (?) *tau* crosses surmounted by a bud, with two dots, one under each of the lateral arms of the cross. From ancient tombs at Akhmîm (Panopolis), Upper Egypt. ? 6th to 9th cent. About 6½ in. square. Bought (242 to 287, 28*l.* 9*s.* 6*d.*).
269.–1887.

SQUARE PANEL (for a linen tunic) of woven tapestry, chiefly red wool and yellow flax. The pattern consists of a trellis with bars on white and small red crosses and green crosses in red discs; in the diamond shapes are foliated cross devices. The woollen threads have been mostly eaten away. From ancient tombs at Akhmîm (Panopolis), Upper Egypt. *? Christian Coptic.* ? 6th to 9th centʸ. 7½ in. square. Bought (242 to 297, 29l. 9s. 6d.). 272.-1887.

SQUARE PANELS (two, fragmentary) of woven tapestry and needlework, coloured wools. In the larger piece is a portion of a king with sceptre in one hand and orb in the other (? Christ), apparently riding—the hind quarters (rudely represented) of his horse only remain. This group was originally set in an inner roundel of the square; about it are Greek letters and small crosses. From ancient tombs at Akhmîm (Panopolis), Upper Egypt. *Christian Coptic.* 6th to 9th centʸ. Various sizes. Given by the Rev. Greville J. Chester. 1656, 1656a.-1888.

The representation of the figures is of a very degraded style. The raised needlework is remarkable.

SKIRT of a linen tunic (part of), with two small medallions of woven tapestry, dark purple wool and yellow flax. Within each medallion on a yellow ground is a small cross device terminated with vine leaves, between which are small roundels and spots. From ancient tombs at Akhmîm (Panopolis), Upper Egypt. ? 6th to 9th centʸ. 2 ft. 7 in. by 18 in. Bought, 1l. 284.-1889.

(*f.*) MEDALLIONS or CIRCULAR PANELS (*orbiculi*) for shoulders and skirts of robes chiefly of the tunic class.

MEDALLION (for a linen robe) of woven tapestry and needlework, brown wool and yellow flax. Within the border, which is edged with the wave device, is a group of three figures: a naked figure of a man in the centre bearing on his left arm a cylindrical casket or *cista;* on each side of him is a seated female, draped and holding up a (?) wreath. From ancient tombs at Akhmîm (Panopolis), Upper Egypt. *Egypto-Roman.* 1st to 5th centʸ. Diam. 4 in. Bought, 1l. 273.-1889.

MEDALLION or CIRCULAR PANEL, wrought into part of a robe of rough towel material (*? gausapum* of the Romans or *kaunakes* of the Greeks), of woven tapestry and needlework, brown wool and yellow flax. A hare is depicted in the inner roundel, which is surrounded by a series of radiating cones; the edge to the medallion is of wave pattern. *Old Egyptian.* ? 1st to 6th centʸ. 9 in. square. Given by C. A. Cookson, Esq., C.B. 111.-1887.

Compare also with No. 760.-1886. See article by Monsieur Heuzey in the "Revue Archéologique," 1887, on the rough-surfaced materials *kaunakes* and *amphi malla.*

MEDALLION or CIRCULAR PANEL (for a tunic) of woven tapestry and needlework, purple wool and flax thread. In the centre are four baskets arranged as a cross, with fishes between them; around these is a border of leaves, amorini, one with a bird, floating women with (?) dishes; this is set in an eight-pointed purple star form; a small roundel with a face in it is in each point of the star. Between the points are small figures in various attitudes. From ancient tombs at Akhmîm (Panopolis), Upper Egypt. *Egypto-Roman.* ? 2nd to 5th centy. Diam. 7 in. Bought, 1*l.* 5*s.* 1279.-1888.

MEDALLION or CIRCULAR PANEL (fragmentary) from a linen tunic of woven tapestry, dark purple and yellow wool on small warps of flax thread. In the centre is a degraded representation of a hunter on horseback with his dog. This group is encircled by a purple band, and beyond this, on a yellow group, are purple animal forms; formerly surrounded by a broad purple band. From ancient tombs at Akhmîm (Panopolis), Upper Egypt. ? 2nd to the 5th centy. W. about 7 in. Bought, 1*l.* 5*s.* 279.-1889.

MEDALLION (a small fragment) of tapestry weaving in coloured wool for a linen tunic. From ancient tombs at Akhmîm (Panopolis), Upper Egypt. ? *Egypto-Roman.* ? 3rd to 6th centy. About 7 in. long. Bought, 7*s.* 1332.-1888.
The colours in this fragment are well preserved.

MEDALLION or CIRCULAR PANEL (for the portion of tunic or cloth No. 348-1890) of woven tapestry, coloured wools and yellow flax. In the centre is a quail and little trefoil plant on a purple ground, enclosed by a border of continuous acanthus scroll set between two yellow bands, and edged by a purple band with tassel ornament. ? *Egypto-Roman.* ? 3rd to 6th centy. Diam. 7¾ in. Bought (with 348.-1890), 12*l.* 347.-1890.
The gradation of tints in the bird is somewhat remarkable.

MEDALLION (to part of tunic skirt) or roundel of woven tapestry, brown wool and yellow flax; with a bird preening itself, and two (?) ears of wheat above it. From ancient tombs at Akhmîm (Panopolis), Upper Egypt. *Egypto-Roman.* ? 3rd to 7th centy. 7¾ in. by 5½ in. Bought, 10*s.* 1312.-1888.

MEDALLION (stitched to a fragment of rough-face towel material *gausapum*) of woven tapestry and needlework, brown wool and yellow flax, with interlacing band ornament. From ancient tombs at Akhmîm (Panopolis), Upper Egypt. ? 3rd to 9th centy. Diam. 2 in. Bought, 5*s.* 1351.-1888.

MEDALLION or CIRCULAR PANEL, very fragmentary (for a linen robe), of woven tapestry, coloured wool, with remains of a rudely-represented group of standing and seated figures, male and female. From ancient tombs at Akhmîm (Panopolis), Upper Egypt. *Christian Coptic.* ? 4th to 6th centy. 4½ in. by 4½ in. Bought (242 to 297, 29*l.* 9*s.* 6*d.*). 278.-1887.

MEDALLION (for a linen robe) of woven tapestry, coloured wool. Within a double circular band, ornamented, is a pair of horsemen discharging arrows at one another as they gallop away in opposite directions; beneath these are two hares, above the spreading stems of a thin and scrolling stem plant device. From ancient tombs at Akhmîm (Panopolis), Upper Egypt. 6th to 9th centy. Diam. 7¼ in. Bought, 6s. 371.–1887.

See similar, but more rudely rendered, figures in portion of hanging No. 276.–1887; also in silk No. 292.–1889; in which latter the bowmen have discharged their arrows into a lion (?). A fragment of similar silk is preserved at the church of St. Servan, Maestricht.

MEDALLION or CIRCULAR PANEL (for a tunic) of woven tapestry, coloured wool, containing on a red ground two nimbed and draped figures, male and female, before a temple (?), and surrounded by a double border, the inner one of a series of yellow, green, and red discs. From ancient tombs at Akhmîm (Panopolis), Upper Egypt. ?Christian Coptic. ?6th to 9th centy. 6½ in. by 5 in. Bought, 1l. 1s. 1283.–1888.

MEDALLION or CIRCULAR PANEL (for a tunic ?) of woven tapestry, coloured wools. The pattern, on a red ground, consists of a central roundel containing a rudely-represented human figure ? seated on a fish; beyond is a balanced arrangement of debased animal and conventional forms. With this is also a small oval piece of similar work. From ancient tombs at Akhmîm (Panopolis), Upper Egypt. ?6th to 9th centy. Diam. 9 in. and 3 in. Bought, 1l. the two.
275, 275a.–1889.

Compare colouring of this with that of No. 352.–1887

MEDALLION or CIRCULAR PANEL (part of) for a tunic, of woven tapestry, coloured wool and flax thread. The pattern originally consisted of a central roundel containing a debased figure. Beyond, in balanced arrangement are rude renderings of two vases, flanked by conventional trees. From ancient tombs at Akhmîm (Panopolis), Upper Egypt. ?Christian Coptic. ?6th to 9th centy. Diam. 7 in. Bought, 7s. 6d. 288.–1889.

(g.) POINTED, OVAL, and OTHER ORNAMENTS for Robes.

TUNIC, part of, to which has been stitched a portion of a small shoulder band (clavus) and an ornamented medallion or roundel (orbiculus) of woven tapestry, brown wool and yellow flax; the finer yellow lines being of needlework. The ornament of the band consists of alternate repetitions of a disc, and a double stem and leaf device enclosing a smaller disc. On each side of the medallion (orbiculus) is a group of vases with balanced vine branches; within the medallion is a horseman galloping with outstretched right hand. From ancient tombs at Akhmîm (Panopolis), Upper Egypt. *Egypto-Roman.* 1st to 5th centy. 10 in. by 4½ in. Bought, 1*l.* 1293.-1888.

Sidonius Apollinaris (5th century) describes Persian stuffs imported into Europe at this time, and specially mentions such equestrian subjects as the one in this roundel. (See Cantor, Lecture II., Egyptian Tapestry, p. 807 of Journal of Society of Arts for 13th September 1889.)

EIGHT-POINTED STAR-SHAPED ORNAMENT (for a robe) of woven tapestry, brown wool and yellow flax. In the centre is a circular band enclosing the half figure of a soldier with cap, carrying a double-bladed axe across his shoulders. Beyond is a radiating arrangement of amphora-shaped vases, from each of which is a double stem leaf device, which intertwists with its neighbour. This arrangement is enclosed in an eight-pointed star-shaped band picked out in outline with an intertwisted double scrolling stem. From ancient tombs at Akhmîm (Panopolis), Upper Egypt. *Egypto-Roman.* ? 1st to 6th centy. 10¼ in. by 10½ in. Bought, 1*l.* 10s. 1272.-1888.

Compare with No. 277.-1889, in which many similar details occur.

ORNAMENT (fragment of, for a linen robe) of woven tapestry and needlework, coloured wool and white flax. This was originally an hexagonal panel with purple border, and white outline guilloche pattern on it, enclosing white ground, on which in colours was a formal and balanced vine device springing from an amphora-shaped vase. From ancient tombs at Akhmîm (Panopolis), Upper Egypt. *Egypto-Roman.* ? 3rd to 6th centy. L. 5½ in. Bought (242 to 297, 29*l.* 9s. 6*d.*). 246.-1887.

ORNAMENT (fragmentary, and originally an octagonal panel for a tunic) of woven tapestry and needlework, coloured wool and flax thread. In the centre on a white ground is a cross in blue with an outline guilloche pattern in white, the spaces between the limbs being occupied by formal trees and birds. Around this is an octagonal border in purple wool worked in outline with a running guilloche band, and edged with petal devices. From ancient tombs at Akmîm (Panopolis), Upper Egypt. ? *Christian Coptic.* 3rd to 6th centy. About 6½ in. by 6 in. Bought (242 to 297, 29*l.* 9s. 6*d.*). 247.-1887.

ORNAMENT (for a linen robe) of woven tapestry, brown wool and yellow flax. Within what was originally **a** pointed oval shape, from which sprang on the outside vine branches, is **an** indented or leaf form, on which is the figure of a nude warrior bearing a shield on his left arm and looking upwards.* From ancient tombs at Akhmîm (Panopolis), Upper Egypt. *Egypto-Roman.* ? 3rd to 6th centy. About 4 in. square. Bought, 10s. 1309.-1888.

* See similar attitude of figures in tunic, No. 631.-1886, pp. 17 and 18 of 1888 Catalogue.

ORNAMENT (fragmentary and originally an octagonal panel for a tunic) of woven tapestry and needlework, coloured wool and flax thread. In the centre, on a white ground, is a purple amphora-shaped vase with ornament in white outline, from which springs a conventional plant with balanced foliage, amongst which are birds. Around this is an octagonal border in purple wool worked in outline with a guilloche band, and edged with petal devices. From ancient tombs at Akhmîm (Panopolis), Upper Egypt. ? *Christian Coptic.* ? 4th to 6th centy. About 6½ in. by 5½ in. Bought (242 to 297, 29*l.* 9*s.* 6*d.*).

245.–1887.

Compare with similar shape panel, 247.–1887.

PENDENT OVAL PANEL and narrow band, from a round ended band (for a linen robe) of woven tapestry, coloured wool with the figure of a lion (?) surrounded by leaf borders. From ancient tombs at Akhmîm (Panopolis), Upper Egypt. ? *Christian Coptic.* ? 4th to 6th centy. About 6 in. by 3 in. Bought (242 to 297, 29*l.* 9*s.* 6*d.*). 280.–1887.

CROSS of woven tapestry, coloured wool, for a linen robe; a long-limbed cross (*patée*) jewelled. From ancient tombs at Akhmîm (Panopolis), Upper Egypt. ? *Christian Coptic.* 4th to 6th centy. W. 5 in. Bought, 7*s.* 1331.–1888.

The various crosses as in Nos. 349.–1887, 245.–1887, 1262.–1888, and 296.–1889 may be compared together.

CROSS of woven tapestry, coloured wool, for a linen robe; a Greek cross jewelled. From ancient tombs at Akhmîm Panopolis), Upper Egypt. *Christian Coptic.* ? 4th to 6th centy. 4¼ in. by 4 in. Bought, 6*s.* 296.–1889.

The various crosses as in Nos. 349.–1887, 245.–1887, 1262.–1888, and 296.–1889 may be compared together.

OVAL ORNAMENT (fragmentary), *vesica*-shaped (for a linen cloth) of woven tapestry and needlework, dark blue wool and yellow flax, filled in with a formal small leaf branch device and scrolls set within a serrated scalloped oval panel. At each opposite end of the outer pointed oval border is a scroll stem, one of which has a small oval panel containing a leaf. From ancient tombs at Akhmîm (Panopolis), Upper Egypt. ? 3rd to 9th centy. About 20 in. by 12 in. Bought, 12*s.*

366.–1887.

ORNAMENT (for a linen robe), of woven tapestry and needlework brown wool and yellow flax, consisting of an eight-pointed star panel, enclosing a roundel picked out in outline with a diaper pattern of square groups of looped stem ornament; within the pointed corners of the star were vine leaves. From ancient tombs at Akhmîm (Panopolis), Upper Egypt. ? 3rd to 9th centy. 12¼ in. by 12 in. Bought (994 to 1216, 91*l.*). 994.–1888.

POINTED OVAL ORNAMENT (part of), for a linen robe, of woven tapestry, brown wool and yellow flax. This consists of a balanced arrangement of two intertwisting formal vine branches. From ancient tombs at Akhmîm (Panopolis), Upper Egypt. ? 3rd to 9th centy. 9 in. by 6 in. Bought, 10*s.* 1313.–1888.

32

OVAL ORNAMENT with short stem, for a linen robe, of woven tapestry, brown wool and flax thread. The oval and stem are edged with tassel devices and brown band enclosing a brown evenly balanced floriated device. From ancient tombs at Akhmîm (Panopolis), Upper Egypt. ? 3rd to 9th centy. 6½ in. by 4¾ in. Given by the Rev. Greville J Chester.

1651.–1888.

ORNAMENT or emblematic badge for a linen robe, of woven tapestry, purple wool. From ancient tombs at Akhmîm (Panopolis), Upper Egypt. ? 3rd to 9th centy. 16 in. by 7½ in. Bought, 4s.

1365.–1888.

See also ornament or badge of two separate oblongs in Nos. 464, 464a.–1889.

ORNAMENT or emblematic badge for a robe, consisting of two small oblongs worked in brown wool with the needle over a ground of yellow wool tapestry weaving. From an ancient Roman cemetery in the Fayûm, Middle Egypt. ? 3rd to 9th centy. 12 in. by 5 in. Bought (with 464a, 3s. the two).

464.–1889.

See also 464a.–1889 and 1365.–1888.

ORNAMENT or emblematic badge for a robe, consisting of two small oblongs of brown wool tapestry weaving, each worked in needlework with border and central device, ? the letter I. From an ancient Roman cemetery in the Fayûm, Middle Egypt. ? 3rd to 9th centy. 7½ in. by 7 in. Bought (with 464, 3s. the two).

464a.–1889.

This sort of badge is to be seen on the robes of ? Abraham entertaining the three angels as represented in mosaic in the Church of Sta. Maria Maggiore, Rome. See also 1365.–1888.

ORNAMENT (part of, for a linen robe) of woven tapestry, coloured wool. The pattern consists of a degraded tree device set within concentric bands, green and red, with yellow waved stem ornament on the green bands. From ancient tombs at Akhmîm (Panopolis), Upper Egypt. ? 6th to 9th centy. 3 in. by 2¾ in. Bought (242 to 297, 29l. 9s. 6d.) 277.–1887

(h.) FRAGMENTS of BANDS, &c. from robes, &c.

FRAGMENT of woven tapestry, coloured wools, with a conventional blossom on a white ground. From ancient tombs at Akhmîm (Panopolis), Upper Egypt. Egypto-Roman. ? 1st to 6th centy. Diam. about 3½ in. Given by the Rev. Greville J. Chester.

354.–1890.

See similar devices in square panels such as No. 712.–1886.

FRAGMENT of woven tapestry, red wool and yellow flax, with a repeated pattern of heart-shaped ornaments or leaves. The wool has mostly perished. From ancient tombs at Akhmîm (Panopolis), Upper Egypt. ? 3rd to 6th centy. 8 in. by 6 in. Bought (242 to 297, 29l. 9s. 6d.). 274.–1887.

FRAGMENT of a band, from a linen robe, of woven tapestry, brown wool and yellow flax. The main portion is of plain brown wool; each edge to it is of narrow waved stem and leaf pattern. From ancient tombs at Akhmîm (Panopolis), Upper Egypt. ? 3rd to 6th centʸ. 5¼ in. by 4¼ in. Bought (994 to 1216, 91*l.*).   998.–1888.

FRAGMENT of woven tapestry, coloured wools, with waved green stem and red blossoms on a black ground. From ancient tombs at Akhmîm (Panopolis), Upper Egypt. ? 3rd to 6th centʸ. 6 in. by 3½ in. Bought, 5s.   301.–1889.

FRAGMENT of woven tapestry, with indications of a pattern of repeated circular white spaces, each filled with either a bunch of grapes or a conventional vine leaf, in coloured wool and white flax. From ancient tombs at Akhmîm (Panopolis), Upper Egypt. ? Egypto-Roman. 4th to 6th centʸ. About 6 in. by 5 in. Bought, 5s.   1345.–1888.

FRAGMENTS (two) of woven tapestry and needlework, brown wool and yellow flax, with lions, &c. and a debased human form. From ancient tombs at Hawara, Middle Egypt. 4th or 5th centʸ. About 6 in. by 4 in. and 5 in. by 4 in. Given by Percy E. Newberry, Esq.   440–440a.–1889.

FRAGMENT of yellow linen, with woven tapestry, brown wool; a small pointed panel* with stem and the foil device in the panel. From ancient tombs at Hawara, Middle Egypt. 4th or 5th centʸ. 7 in. by 3 in. Given by Percy E. Newberry, Esq.   441.–1889.

* Probably the pendent panel from a rounded ended band or *clavus.*

FRAGMENT of woven tapestry and needlework, brown wool and yellow flax. From ancient tombs at Hawara, Middle Egypt. 4th or 5th centʸ. 9 in. by 5 in. Given by Percy E. Newberry, Esq.   443.–1889.

FRAGMENT of linen, with a floriated cross on a red panel of woven tapestry in green and yellow ground. From ancient tombs at Hawara, Middle Egypt. 4th or 5th centʸ. 2 in. by 2 in. Given by Percy E. Newberry, Esq.   444.–1889.

FRAGMENT of yellow linen, with end of a narrow band of leafy scroll pattern of woven tapestry, brown wool. From ancient tombs at Hawara, Middle Egypt. 4th or 5th centʸ. 5½ in. by 2 in. Given by Percy E. Newberry, Esq.   445.–1889.

FRAGMENT of linen, with remnants, ornamental stripes (degraded details, ? leaf-shapes, with faces and stems) in woven tapestry, coloured wool, and yellow flax. From ancient tombs at Akhmîm (Panopolis), Upper Egypt. ? 6th to 9th centʸ. 9 in. by 3 in. Bought (242 to 297, 29*l.* 9*s.* 6*d.*).   260.–1887.

o 69191.   C

FRAGMENT of woven tapestry, red and black wool with a pattern of wavy stems and foliated circular devices between them. To this a piece of a narrower band with waved stem and leafy devices is attached. From ancient tombs at Akhmîm (Panopolis), Upper Egypt. ?6th to 9th cent⁷. 4 in. square. Bought (242 to 297, 29l. 9s. 6d.). 267.–1887.

FRAGMENT of an oblong band of woven tapestry in black, red, yellow, and white coloured wool. From ancient tombs at Akhmîm (Panopolis), Upper Egypt. ?6th to 9th cent⁷. 8¾ in. by 6½ in. Bought (242 to 297, 29l. 9s. 6d.).

268.–1887.

FRAGMENT of linen with a band of small floral and fruit ornaments, scattered over it, of woven tapestry, coloured wool, and similar devices on ground beyond the band. From ancient tombs at Akhmîm (Panopolis), Upper Egypt. ?6th to 9th cent⁷. About 9 in. by 8 in. Bought (242 to 297, 29l. 9s. 6d.).

283.–1887.

See also note to 1363.–1888.

FRAGMENT of linen robe with a group of large, spreading (?) bud and stem devices and small petal forms arranged in balanced order about a central circular panel edged with wave ornament and containing a blossom and cross *pattée* device. These are of woven tapestry, chiefly red wools with small portions of yellow and green wool. From ancient tombs at Akhmîm (Panopolis), Upper Egypt. ?6th to 9th cent⁷. About 9¼ in. by 8½ in. Bought (242 to 297, 29l. 9s. 6d.). 285.–1887.

The larger (?) bud devices almost suggest the old Egyptian device of the disc and horns as seen on Isis and Hathor.

FRAGMENT of linen robe with a group of large, spreading (?) bud and stem devices and small petal forms arranged in balanced order about a central circular panel edged with wave ornament and containing a blossom and cross *pattée* device. These are of woven tapestry, chiefly red wools with small portions of yellow and green wool. From ancient tombs at Akhmîm (Panopolis), Upper Egypt. ?6th to 9th cent⁷. About 12 in. by 11 in. Bought (242 to 297, 29l. 9s. 6d.). 285a.–1887.

The larger (?) bud devices almost suggest the old Egyptian device of the disc and horns as seen on Isis and Hathor.

FRAGMENT of linen with a row of detached leaf ornaments flanked on each side by a row of small circle and stem symbols of woven tapestry, coloured wool, the central row chiefly blue, the others red. From ancient tombs at Akhmîm (Panopolis), Upper Egypt. ?6th to 9th cent⁷. 13 in. by 5 in. Bought (242 to 297, 29l. 9s. 6d.). 286.–1887.

See note to No. 1362.–1888.

FRAGMENT of linen with a band of small floral and fruit ornaments scattered over it, of woven tapestry, coloured wool, and edged with a strip of blue woollen material on which is a pattern of alternating crosses and diamonds in white. From ancient tombs at Akhmîm (Panopolis), Upper Egypt. 6th to 9th cent. About 9 in. by 5 in. Bought (242 to 297, 29l. 9s. 6d.). 288.-1887.

See also note to No. 1363.-1888.

FRAGMENT of coarse linen, ornamented with two flower or leaf forms, woven tapestry, coloured wool. From ancient tombs at Akhmîm (Panopolis), Upper Egypt. 6th to 9th cent. About 16 in. by 7½ in. Given by the Rev. Greville J. Chester.
302.-1887.

FRAGMENT of a looped-surfaced, woven linen cloth with part of a band of woven tapestry, coloured wool and yellow flax. The ornamentation of the band appears to have consisted of a waved stem, with either an animal or a floral device alternately in each wave. From ancient tombs at Akhmîm (Panopolis), Upper Egypt. ?6th to 9th cent. About 12 in. square. Bought, 10s. 448.-1887.

See similar coarse tapestry weaving in No. 1327.-1888 and 1278, 1278c.-1888.

FRAGMENT of linen with a large leaf shape filled in on a dark ground with a rudely-rendered blossoming plant; beyond it is a group of small blossom devices, all of woven tapestry, coloured wools. From ancient tombs at Akhmîm (Panopolis), Upper Egypt. ?6th to 9th cent. About 7 in. by 6 in. Bought, 5s. 1343.-1888.

See note to 1363.-1888.

FRAGMENT of linen with a spotted pattern of small and larger leaf devices, arranged as a band, of woven tapestry, coloured wools. From ancient tombs at Akhmîm (Panopolis), Upper Egypt. ?6th to 9th cent. 7 in. by 4 in. Given by the Rev. Greville J. Chester. 1652.-1888.

See note to 1363.-1888.

BAND, fragment of, with portion of a narrow band containing continuous waved stem and leaf ornament and other detached devices of woven tapestry, coloured wools, inwoven into the linen. From ancient tombs at Akhmîm (Panopolis), Upper Egypt. ? 6th to 9th cent. 5 in. by 1¾ in. Bought, 5s.
1353.-1888.

See note to 1363.-1888. This is a portion of band No. 1341.-1888.

FRAGMENT of linen with tapestry-woven narrow stem and petal ornament in coloured wool. From ancient tombs at Akhmîm (Panopolis), Upper Egypt. ?6th to 9th cent. 12½ in. by 4 in. Bought, 5s. 1359.-1888.

This is somewhat similar in style to ornament on No. 634.-1886, but ruder in work.

FRAGMENT of linen with a narrow, dark-coloured band ornamented with little floral devices in colours and flanked by separated repeated small leaf devices of woven tapestry, coloured wool, inwoven into linen. From ancient tombs at Akhmîm (Panopolis), Upper Egypt. ?6th to 9th cent. 10½ in. by 2½ in. Bought, 5s. 1361.-1888.

See note to 1363.-1888.

FRAGMENT of linen with a spotted pattern of small separated floral devices and triple leafy stems in woven tapestry, coloured wools. From ancient tombs at Akhmîm (Panopolis), Upper Egypt. ? 6th to 9th cent'. 6 in. by 3 in. Bought, 5s.
1363.-1888.

Linens ornamented in this way with separated details woven into them appear from the ornamental character of the details to belong to a later period than that from 1st to 6th cent'. At that period it seems to have been the fashion to weave or work the ornamentation of the linens into panels, bands, &c. Beyond and about the panels or bands was plain linen. Some of the robes, displayed in the Ravenna Mosaics of the Emperor Justinian and the Empress Theodora with their suites, are ornamented with separated or detached details scattered in diaper patterns over them. On the other hand, such diaper patterns on linen, the details being of tapestry-weaving, as well as bands of such weaving, were in vogue in the 3rd or 4th centuries B.C., as may be concluded from fragments of linen ornamented with tapestry-woven diaper pattern of ducks, which are deposited in the Museum of the Hermitage at St. Petersburg. These fragments with other relics of Greek or Græco-Scythian Art were discovered in the tomb of the Seven Brothers at Temriouck, formerly a Greek settlement in the province of Kouban on the north-eastern shores of the Black Sea.

FRAGMENT of linen with repeated pairs of leaves and separate other devices (debased in character) of woven tapestry, coloured wool, inwoven into linen. From ancient tombs at Akhmîm (Panopolis), Upper Egypt. ? 6th to 9th cent'. 12 in. by 1¼ in. Bought, 5s.   1362.-1888.
See note to 1363.-1888.

FRAGMENT of fine linen with a band of woven tapestry and needlework, fine black wool and yellow flax, and another band, towards the fringe of the fragment, of yellow silk. From ancient tombs at Akhmîm (Panopolis), Upper Egypt. ? 6th to 9th cent'. About 8 in. by 5 in. Bought, 2s. 6d.
1376.-1888.

FRAGMENT of linen, with tapestry-woven fruit or flowers in coloured wool. From ancient tombs at Akhmîm (Panopolis), Upper Egypt. 6th to 9th cent'. L. 7 in. Given by the Rev. Greville J. Chester.   1653.-1888.

FRAGMENT (? band from a robe) of woven tapestry, faded brown, blue, green, and yellow wools, with a degraded pattern of crosses or degraded four petal devices within shaped panels. From ancient tombs at Akhmîm (Panopolis), Upper Egypt. ? 6th to 9th cent'. 7½ in. by 6 in. Given by the Rev. Greville J. Chester.   1657.-1888.

FRAGMENT probably of a circular panel, for a robe, of woven tapestry, faded coloured wools, degraded details. From ancient tombs at Akhmîm (Panopolis), Upper Egypt. ? 6th to 9th cent'. About 4 in. by 3 in. Given by the Rev. Greville J. Chester.   1659.-1888.

FRAGMENT (? of a cloth or robe) of woven tapestry in brown, green, and yellow wools, with various ornamental devices, deteriorated. From ancient tombs at Akhmîm (Panopolis), Upper Egypt. ? 6th to 9th cent'. About 11 in. by 4 in Given by the Rev. Greville J. Chester.   1667.-1888

FRAGMENT of coarse linen, with bands of tapestry weaving and portions of darning with coloured wools. From ancient tombs at Akhmîm (Panopolis), Upper Egypt. ? 6th to 9th centy. L. about 7 in. Given by the Rev. Greville J. Chester.

261.–1889.

FRAGMENT (of a cloth) of woven tapestry, coloured wool and white flax. The ornament consisted of a central stem with close-lying leaves on each side of it. From ancient tombs at Akhmîm (Panopolis), Upper Egypt. ? 6th to 9th centy. 6 in. by 5 in. Given by the Rev. Greville J. Chester. 266.–1889.
See larger specimens of similar style of coarse tapestry weaving in Nos. 1327.–1888.

FRAGMENT of linen, with woven tapestry bird in coloured wool. From ancient tombs at Akhmîm (Panopolis), Upper Egypt. ? 6th to 9th centy. 3½ in. by 2 in. Bought, 5s. 300.–1889.

FRAGMENT of linen with a double band of woven tapestry in red wool on which are oval forms in yellow, outlined with black. From ancient tombs at Hawara, Middle Egypt. ? 6th to 9th centy. 7¼ in. by 2½ in. Given by Percy E. Newberry, Esq. 442.–1889.

FRAGMENT (probably the small circular panel of a round ended band or clavus for a tunic) of woven tapestry, coloured wool, with the debased rendering of a goose and a boy ? surrounded by a border. From an ancient Roman cemetery in the Fayûm, Middle Egypt. ? 6th to 9th centy. H. 3½ in., W. 2½ in. Given by W. M. Flinders Petrie, Esq. 458.–1889.

FRAGMENT of coarse linen cloth with inserted ornaments of woven tapestry, coloured wool, showing a representation of a cat and part of a floral device. From an ancient Roman cemetery in the Fayûm, Middle Egypt. ? 6th to 9th centy. About 10 in. by 5 in. Bought, 12s. 482.–1889.

FRAGMENTS (four) of linen with small stripes or bands of woven tapestry, coloured silks. From ancient tombs at Akhmîm (Panopolis), Upper Egypt. ? Saracenic. 7th to 11th centy. Various sizes. Bought, 10s. the four. 291 to 291c.–1889.

(i.) CLOTHS, WRAPPERS, and HANGINGS, &c.

CLOTH (portion of) of linen, with a series of four parallel bands of woven tapestry and needlework, purple and yellow wool and white flax. The main grounds of these several bands are covered with angular key patterns with repeated looped stem devices, with hexagonal, square, and lozenge forms, with cross bars forming various angular figures. The small border- ings on each side of the main grounds consist (1) of waved stem, leaf, and berry devices, (2) of double intercrossing waved stem and leaf devices between them, (3) of waved stem with leaf and berry devices, and (4) of repeated vertical leaf forms. From ancient tombs at Akhmîm (Panopolis), Upper Egypt. ? Egypto-Roman. ? 1st to 6th centy. 4 ft. by 2 ft. 3½ in. Bought, 1l. 10s. 360.–1887.

CLOTH (part of) with two narrow bands of continuous leafy ornament, between which is a dolphin in tapestry weaving of brown wool and white flax. From ancient tombs at Akhmîm (Panopolis), Upper Egypt. *Egypto-Roman.* 1st to 6th centy. 14½ in. by 7 in. Bought, 10s. 1302.–1888.

This is noticeable for the introduction of the dolphin frequently used in classical and Christian ornamentation.

CLOTH (part of) of rough towel material, faced with looped linen tufts with indications of a band formerly of woven tapestry coloured wools ; at one end of the band is a yellow cross pattée on dark blue ground. From ancient tombs at Akhmîm (Panopolis), Upper Egypt. ? 3rd to 6th centy. 13 in. by 11 in. Bought (242 to 297, 29l. 9s. 6d.). 270.–1887.

CLOTH OF LINEN, portion of, with double waved stem and vine leaf border, and a pointed oval shape of formally-arranged vine leaves, grapes, and branches, with long stem, of woven tapestry, purple wool, and white flax. From ancient tombs at Akhmîm (Panopolis), Upper Egypt. 3rd to 6th centy. About 20 in. by 17 in. Bought, 1l. 1294.–1888.

CLOTH of linen, fringed, with two parallel bands of woven tapestry in purple wool and flax. From ancient tombs at Akhmîm (Panopolis), Upper Egypt. 3rd to 6th centy. 4 ft. 5 in. by 20 in. Bought, 10s. 286.–1889.

CLOTH (part of) of linen, with a band of woven tapestry and needlework, brown and yellow wools and white flax. Along the band in outline is a counterchanging pattern of zigzags and looped stems ; at one end is a yellow bird on a brown ground. From ancient tombs at Akhmîm (Panopolis), Upper Egypt. *Egypto-Roman.* ? 3rd to 6th centy. L. 2 ft. 2 in., W. 9 in. Bought, 1l. 5s. 254.–1890.

See also 255.–1890.

CLOTH (part of) of linen, with two bands of woven tapestry and needlework, brown and yellow wools and white flax. Along the bands in outline is a repeated diagonally set key ornament ; at the end of one of the bands is a yellow bird on a brown ground. From ancient tombs at Akhmîm (Panopolis), Upper Egypt. *Egypto-Roman.* ? 3rd to 6th centy. L. 22 in., W. 13 in. Bought, 1l. 5s. · 255.–1890.

See also 254.–1880.

END of a cloth of linen, with ornaments of woven tapestry, coloured wools, chiefly red, purple, and green. Between two bands of twisted red and green stems are four *tau* crosses surmounted by four discs, on each of which are either a cross and four spots, stars, or the cipher XP. Above, to the right, is another *tau* cross and disc with spots in it. From ancient tombs at Akhmîm (Panopolis), Upper Egypt. *Christian Coptic.* 4th or 5th centy. 13 in. by 12 in. Bought, 2l. 258.–1890.

The *tau* cross and disc conjoined is a very ancient, well-known, pagan Egyptian symbol (*crux ansata*) typifying productiveness. Its use here in conjunction with Christian symbols is especially interesting.

CLOTH (portion of) of linen, with three rows of detached leaves and coloured spots of woven tapestry, wool. From ancient tombs at Akhmîm (Panopolis), Upper Egypt. ?6th to 9th centy. About 2 ft. 1 in. by 18 in. Bought (242 to 297, 29l. 9s. 6d.). 287.–1887.
See note to 1368.—1888.

CLOTH (portion of) of linen, with woven tapestry, coloured wool ornament and border. The pattern consists of an arrangement of circular blossoms into a trellis, within the spaces of which are remains of tree and fruit devices. The border has a repeated pattern of small floral and bud devices. From ancient tombs at Akhmîm (Panopolis), Upper Egypt. ? 6th to 9th centy. 2 ft. 11 in. by 12 in. Bought (242 to 297, 29l. 9s. 6d.). 289.–1887.

CLOTH (end of) of red wool ; along one end in woven tapestry and needlework are two star-shape panels, and ? a crux ansata between them connected by a narrow strip with wave stem and leaf devices. From ancient tombs at Akhmîm (Panopolis), Upper Egypt. 6th to 9th centy. 23 in. by 12 in. Bought, 12s. 450.–1887.

CLOTH (end of) of lightish brown wool, with a medallion of woven tapestry and needlework in darker wool, and with a diaper filling of geometrical forms worked in yellow outline with the needle. From ancient tombs at Akhmîm (Panopolis), Upper Egypt. ? 6th to 9th centy. 21 in. by 17½ in. Bought, 16s. 1295.–1888.

CLOTH (fragment of) of woven tapestry, coloured wools (chiefly dark blue and white) with alternate stripes, either plain blue or figured in colours on white. From ancient tombs at Akhmîm (Panopolis), Upper Egypt. 6th to 9th centy. About 11 in. by 9 in. Bought, 7s. 6d. 289.–1889.

CLOTH (part of) of red and purple woollen stuff, with a band of woven tapestry and needlework, purple and yellow wool, with ornament of leafy and scroll devices, and small dark panels set with yellow blossoms? From an ancient Roman cemetery in the Fayûm, Middle Egypt. ?6th to 9th centy. 2 ft. 10 in. by 23 in. Bought, 1l. 474.–1889.

CLOTH (end of) of brown and yellow wool, woven with a diaper pattern of birds in octagonal medallions and small blossoms between the octagons. At the two ends are two square panels of fine warp of woven tapestry and needlework in purple and yellow wools with guilloche patterns in fine outline on them. The ends are bound by yellowish cords, and the sides are fringed. From ancient tombs at Akhmîm (Panopolis), Upper Egypt. Egypto-Byzantine ? 6th to 9th centy ? 2 ft. 2 in. by 17 in. Bought, 2l. 2s. 243.–1890.

CLOTH (part of) of linen ; applied to one side are a large medallion and two bands of woven tapestry and needlework, purple wool and white flax. The pattern on the medallion, in outline, consists of a diapering of squares, diamonds and circles, &c.; that of the bands consists of two stems intertwined with leaf and fruit forms in the large intervening spaces. Worked into the other side with coloured wools in needlework of closely-lying loops is a medallion decorated with a band in white, red, and green, and a central square divided into nine small squares of green and red alternating. The end is fringed. From ancient tombs at Akhmîm (Panopolis), Upper Egypt. 6th to 9th cent^y. 2 ft. 8½ in. by 2 ft. 3½ in. Given by the Rev. Greville J. Chester.   358.–1890.

HANGING (portion of) of woven tapestry, coloured wools. The ornamentation consists of a series of horizontal leafy bands or garlands and other devices; between the three upper bands on a red ground is a grotesque rendering of a bird on a leafy twig. The lower part of the hanging is ornamented with ornamental bands arranged closely together, in lowest of which is a rose blossom device. From ancient tombs at Akhmîm (Panopolis), Upper Egypt. *? Egypto-Roman.* 3rd to 6th cent^y 5 ft. 3 in. by 19¾ in. Bought, 5*l*. 267.–1889.

HANGING (portion of) of woven tapestry, coloured wools. Part of a leafy band and bird are shown. From ancient tombs at Akhmîm (Panopolis), Upper Egypt. *? Egypto-Roman.* 3rd to 6th cent^y. 14½ in. by 14 in. Bought, 1*l*.   268.–1889.

See more complete specimen, No. 267.–1889.

HANGING (part of) of linen, with woven tapestry ornament in coloured wool, consisting of a flying female figure, draped and wearing a jewelled diadem, and supporting with outstretched arms part of a wreath encircling part of a jewelled Greek cross, a dove ?, and the letter alpha. From ancient tombs at Akhmîm (Panopolis), Upper Egypt. *Christian Coptic.* 4th to 6th cent^y. 2 ft. 2 in. by 13 in. Bought (349 to 358, 100*l*.).   349.–1887.

Similar figures are sculptured on the thrones of Rustem at Kermanchah in Persia. Those are of the Sassanian period (3rd to 7th cent^y). On ivory diptychs of the 6th cent^y and of later Roman and Byzantine character there are similar angels and wreathed crosses. The pose of this figure and its treatment as an ornamental or decorative device are in accordance with those of a typical and similar device freely used by Roman sculptors of the 1st cent^y.

HANGING (part of), stitched to coarse linen, of woven tapestry, red wool and white flax thread, with pattern of repeated roundels with waved stem and leaf borders, each enclosing a degraded rendering of a group of two horsemen with heads turned towards one another and shooting arrows with bows; beneath them two animals (see similar group in 1284.–1888). The head of one of the men in each group is rayed. Between the roundels are formal devices of stem and leaf ornament. From ancient tombs at Akhmîm (Panopolis), Upper Egypt. ? 6th to 9th cent^y. 3 ft. by 7½ in. Bought (242 to 297, 29*l*. 9s. 6*d*.).   276.–1887.

See notes to Nos. 1284.–1888 and 417.–1887.

HANGING (fragment of) of woven tapestry, coloured wool threads over a flax warp. The ground is red, and the ornament consists of repeated circles or roundels and portions of roundels with ornamented borders, enclosing various groups of figures on foot and on horseback, and animals; in one of the roundels are the remains of a (?) Greek inscription. Between the roundels are small square and star devices. From ancient tombs at Akhmîm (Panopolis), Upper Egypt. ? *Christian Coptic.* 6th to 9th cent?. About 2 ft. by 8 in. Given by C. Purdon Clarke, Esq., C.I.E. 417.-1887

This special class of pattern with repeated roundels is frequently seen in Byzantine pattern textiles of the 9th and later centuries. See silks (Nos. 292.-1889, 8233.-1863, &c.).

HANGING (portion of) of woven tapestry, crimson wool and white flax, with a trellis enclosing diamond-shaped spaces, within each of which is either a medallion with debased balanced ornament or a square and quatrefoil combined, in centre of which is a cross. From ancient tombs at Akhmîm (Panopolis). Upper Egypt. ?6th to 9th cent?. About 15 in. by 13 in. Bought, 13s. 364.-1887.

See also 896.-1886 and 282-1889.

HANGING (fragment of) of woven tapestry, red and brown wool over a flax warp. The ground is brown, and the ornament consists of repeated roundels and portions of roundels with variously ornamented borders, enclosing pairs of horsemen and animals beneath them. Between the roundels are small blossom devices. From ancient tombs at Akhmîm (Panopolis), Upper Egypt. ? 6th to 9th cent?. 2 ft. 9 in. by 9 in. Bought, 1*l.* 1s. 1284.-1888.

This special class of pattern with repeated roundels is frequently seen in Byzantine figured textiles of the 9th and later centuries (see silks Nos. 292.-1889, 8233.-1863, and tapestry-woven specimens 417.-1887 and 276.-1887).

HANGING (part of) of woven tapestry, red wool and white flax, with pattern of repeated roundels, with degraded ornamental borders enclosing a degraded rendering of two horsemen confronting one another, their horses' heads turned outwards. One horseman has a double-bladed axe, the other is shooting an arrow from a bow; beneath the horsemen are small animals. Between the roundels are formal devices of stem and leaf ornament. From ancient tombs at Akhmîm (Panopolis), Upper Egypt. ? 6th to 9th cent?. 23 in. by 9 in. Bought, 1*l.* 1287.-1888.

See note to 1284.-1888 and 417.-1887.

HANGING (portion of) of woven tapestry, crimson wool, and white flax, with a trellis enclosing, in separate diamond or lozenge-shaped spaces, pointed ovals with leafy stem ornament, and quatrefoils with crosses in each foil and in the centre of them. From ancient tombs at Akhmîm (Panopolis), Upper Egypt. ? 6th to 9th cent?. 3 ft. by 13½ in. Bought, 1*l.* 10s. 282.-1889.

See also 896.-1886.

HANGING or CLOTH of coarse linen with border and insertions
of woven tapestry, coloured wools. The ornament of the
border consists of a series of oval panels, each containing a
fruit (pomegranate), or flower (lotus, tulip, &c.). On the main
ground is ? a fanciful cypress tree form, or ? a flabellum, and a
number of ? small lotus flowers, distributed at regular intervals.
From an ancient Roman cemetery in the Fayûm, Middle
Egypt. ? 6th to 9th centy. 3 ft. 6 in. by about 15 in. Given
by H. M. Kennard, Esq. 318.–1889.
See also note to 1363.–1888.

(j.) BANDS and SQUARES for CLOTHS.

SQUARE PANEL (? for a cloth) of woven tapestry, purple and
coloured wools and white flax. The pattern consists of a
square border of linked roundels, in each of which is either a
vine leaf, a duck, or star device ; within the square border are
four larger linked roundels; in the two upper ones is a
kneeling man apparently throwing a stone, and a (?) panther
confronting him ; in the two lower ones is a kneeling man
with a spear and a (?) lion or tiger running at him. Between
these four roundels are green and red cruciform leaf devices.
From ancient tombs at Akhmîm (Panopolis), Upper Egypt.
Egypto-Roman. ? 1st to 6th centy. 14½ in. square. Bought
(242 to 297, 29l. 9s. 6d.). 243.–1887.

SQUARE PANEL (? for a cloth) of woven tapestry, brown and
coloured wools and yellow flax. The pattern consists of a
square border of linked roundels, in each of which is a
grotesque animal; within the square border is a central
roundel containing a bird, (?) red-legged partridge with yellow
wing and tail, and a conventional leafy spray in its beak.
From ancient tombs at Akhmîm (Panopolis), Upper Egypt.
Egypto-Roman. 1st to 6th centy. 9 in. by 8 in. Bought,
1l. 15s. 1268.–1888.

SQUARE PANEL (fragmentary)? for a cloth, of woven tapestry,
coloured wools and white flax. In the centre are interlaced
bands forming four spaces, in each of which is a basket of
fruit (? calathus) ; between the spaces are trefoil devices ; the
whole is set within a square border of inter-crossing waved
yellow bands, between which, alternately, are red and blue
blossoms. From ancient tombs at Akhmîm (Panopolis), Upper
Egypt. Egypto-Roman. 1st to 6th centy. 9 in. by 8½ in.
Bought, 1l. 276.–1889.

SQUARE PANEL (? for a cloth) of woven tapestry and needlework,
fine-coloured wools on small flax warp threads. The pattern
consists of alternate groups of rose plant and vines framed in
an intertwining border of dark blue wool, worked with a
guilloche pattern in whitish threads; in the centre is a red
rose blossom. The square border of the whole piece is of
purple wool worked with a guilloche pattern in whitish

threads. From ancient tombs at Akhmîm (Panopolis), Upper Egypt. *Egypto-Roman?* 1st to 6th centy. 10 in. square. Bought, 2*l*. 2*s*.   261.–1890.

SQUARE PANEL (for a cloth of rough towel material) of woven tapestry and needlework, purple and white flax. The outer border of the panel consists of acanthus leaf scroll, purple on white; within this a square border of guilloche ornament in white outline on purple ground, and within this a radiating group of four amphora-shaped vases with diagonal floriated stems, purple on white, and a small white cross in centre. From ancient tombs at Akhmîm (Panopolis), Upper Egypt. *? Egypto-Roman.* 3rd to 6th centy. 13 in. by 12 in. Bought (with 1271*a*, Band), 1*l*. 10*s*. the two.   1271.–1888.

BAND (narrow, fragmentary, ? for end of a friezed cloth) of tapestry weaving, red wool and yellow flax. The ornament consists of a central white leafy stem and flower or fruit device on red ground, and on each side of it a continuous waved stem and leaf ornament, edged with waved pattern. From ancient tombs at Akhmîm (Panopolis), Upper Egypt. *Egypto-Roman.* 1st to 6th centy. 12 in. by 3 in. Bought, 7*s*.   1333.–1888.

BAND (part of) for a cloth or cover, of woven tapestry, coloured wools and yellow flax, with continuous pattern of nude, or semi-nude, figures holding up vases, arranged to enclose a diamond panel, in the centre of each of which was a medallion with a pair of birds on it. Beyond and between the diamond panels are the halves of blossom ornaments. A border of four small stripes runs along the sides. From ancient tombs at Akhmîm (Panopolis), Upper Egypt. *? Egypto-Roman.* 3rd to 6th centy. 12 in. by 6 in. Bought (242 to 297, 29*l*. 9*s*. 6*d*.).   273.–1887.

BORDER (? for a cloth, fragment) of woven tapestry, coloured wool and yellow flax. The pattern consists of an acanthus leaf scroll, in which are introduced a lion and another animal, possibly a hound, alternating with figures of a draped female, dancing, and a warrior with a shield: around these is a rectangular border of waved stem and ivy leaf pattern. From ancient tombs at Akhmîm (Panopolis), Upper Egypt. 3rd to 6th centy. 23 in. by 10 in. Bought (349 to 358, 100*l*.).   351.–1887.

BAND (for a cloth of rough towel material) of woven tapestry, purple and red wool and white flax. The pattern consists of an acanthus leaf scroll with birds, animals, fruit, and leafy sprays in the intervening spaces; the birds have red beaks and legs, and the animals red tongues. From ancient tombs at Akhmîm (Panopolis), Upper Egypt. *? Christian Coptic.* 3rd to 6th centy. 2 ft. 10 in. by 8 in. wide. Bought (with 1271, square panel), 1*l*. 10*s*. the two.   1271*a*.–1888.

SQUARE PANEL (? for a cloth) of woven tapestry, brown wool and yellow flax. In the centre is a white roundel within a brown square; in the roundel a lion. Around the square is a zig-zag trellis ornament, edged with tassel devices. From ancient tombs at Akhmîn (Panopolis), Upper Egypt. *Egypto-Roman.* ? 3rd to 6th cent. 10 in. by 8¼ in. Bought, 1*l.* 10*s.*

1273.–1888.

BAND (? for a cloth, six fragments), of woven tapestry, coloured wool and yellow flax. Portions of draped figures (male and female) and of animals are set within borders of waved, thin stem and ivy leaf pattern. From ancient tombs at Akhmîm (Panopolis), Upper Egypt. ? *Egypto-Roman.* 3rd to 6th cent. Various dimensions. Bought, 1*l.* 10*s.* the six.

1278 to 1278e.–1888.

BAND (for end of a fringed cloth) of woven tapestry, red wool and yellow flax. The pattern consists of a centre square containing a circular band, within which is a rudely rendered animal; on each side are double bands of repeated scroll and trefoil devices; edged with continuous wave pattern. From ancient tombs at Akhmîm (Panopolis), Upper Egypt. 3rd to 6th cent. 12 in. by 8½ in. Bought, 1*l.* 1291.–1888.

Compare with No. 282.–1887.

BORDER AND PANELS (for a linen cloth, one end only) of woven tapestry, brown wool and yellow flax. The horizontal band or border has two short bands at right angles to each end of it. They are terminated with a narrow stem and leaf device within which is a cross. Along the whole border is a series of blossoms and small circular devices alternated. On the ground of the cloth and near the inner right angles are two square and quatrefoil panels, with birds at the angles, and groups of little circle devices within roundels at the quatrefoils. The centre of each panel has a brown sea-horse (hippo camp) on a yellow ground. The cloth has a fragment of its fringe. From ancient tombs at Akhmîm (Panopolis), Upper Egypt. ? 3rd to 9th cent. 20 in. by 10½ in. Bought, 10*s.* 1301.–1888.

BORDER (? for a linen robe or cloth) of woven tapestry and needlework, purple-brown wool and yellow flax. The main border having two turned ends is filled in with squares and circles alternated, each containing a different variety of interlacing narrow band pattern; these are set within a narrow border of circle and blossom devices. From each of the turned ends of the border are three larger and two smaller pendent bands of various interlacing narrow band patterns. From an ancient Roman cemetery in the Fayûm, Middle Egypt. ? 3rd to 6th cent. L. 4 ft. 7 in., W. 6 in. Bought, 5*l.*

462.–1889.

BORDER (? for a cloth, portion), of woven tapestry, coloured wool, with a repeated group of bowl of fruit with a bird on either side of it and a garland or festoon beneath ; along the top, square and circular forms of different kinds are repeated. Towards the right hand is a jewelled cross with four human faces between the limbs, and a bird on each side of the upper limb of the Cross. From ancient tombs at Akhmîm (Pano polis), Upper Egypt. ? *Christian Coptic.* 4th to 6th centʸ. 2 ft. 9½ in. by 6¾ in. Bought (349 to 358, 100*l.*).

350.-1887.

See also crosses in 349.-1887, 245.-1887, 1262.-1888, and 296.-1889.

SQUARE PANEL (? for a cloth) of woven tapestry and needle-work, brown and yellow wools and yellow flax. The central roundel containing a grotesque spotted animal (? a dog) is surrounded by two yellow bands, between which are white discs on a brown ground. Beyond this are rectangular corner bands with alternate circles of (?) grapes and vine leaves. The white spandrils within these borders have each a brown triple-leaf device. From ancient tombs at Akhmîm (Panopolis), Upper Egypt. ? 1st to 6th centʸ. 9 in. square. Bought, 1*l.*

271.-1889.

Compare with 639.-1886.

BAND (part of, for a cloth) of woven tapestry, brown wool and white flax. The pattern consists of repeated similar groups of degraded ornament separated by a strip of white ground with brown details, and edged with waved stem and triple-tongue device in white on brown. From ancient tombs at Akhmîm (Panopolis), Upper Egypt. ? 6th to 9th centʸ. 9 in. by 4 in. Bought (242 to 297, 29*l.* 9*s.* 6*d.*). 252.-1887.

BROAD BAND (fragment of) for a cloth (?), of woven tapestry, coloured wool. The pattern originally consisted of a series of large and small medallions surrounded by bands of leaf and petal devices and filled in with balanced arrangements of rudely rendered animal and human forms, floral and other forms on a crimson ground. From ancient tombs at Akhmîm (Panopolis), Upper Egypt. ? 6th to 9th centʸ. About 12 in. square. Bought (349 to 358, 100*l.*). 352.-1887.

Anastasius Bibliothecarius (9th century) describes the pattern of dresses in which such medallions or wheels appear, " *Vestem cum rotis.*"

BAND (part of, from a cloth ?) of woven tapestry, coloured wool. The design consists of a waved stem with fruit (pomegranates) and ? tulips. From ancient tombs at Akhmîm (Panopolis), Upper Egypt. ? 6th to 9th centʸ. 20 in. by 3 in. Bought, 7*s.* 6*d.* 1327.-1888.

BAND or strip of dark purple woollen cloth with a narrow band of woven tapestry, yellow and purple wool, containing a waved stem and vine leaf pattern. From ancient tombs at Akhmîm (Panopolis), Upper Egypt. ? 6th to 9th centʸ. 5 ft. 1 in. by 3 in. Bought, 10*s.* 293.-1889.

BORDERS (five fragments of, for a red woollen cloth) of woven tapestry, yellow and dark brown wools. The pattern consists of a central double stem, with pointed oval openings at regular intervals, in which are debased renderings of birds and vases, human heads, and small animals. This central double stem lies across and divides a succession of roundels into two parts, each part containing a man and woman two mounted horsemen and dogs grotesquely rendered. The whole is edged on both sides with pattern of linked small roundels in which are small debased human figures. From an ancient Roman cemetery in the Fayûm, Middle Egypt. ? 6th to 9th cent.ʸ Irregular shapes and sizes. Given by W. M. Flinders Petrie, Esq.   451–451d.–1889.

BAND (part of, for a blue woollen cloth) of woven tapestry, purple wool and yellow flax. The pattern consists of an orderly and balanced arrangement of debased conventional floral and animal forms. From an ancient Roman cemetery in the Fayûm, Middle Egypt. ? 6th to 9th cent.ʸ. 4 ft. by 12½ in. Bought, 15s.   478.–1889.

Compare the style of this ornament with that in the piece of blue and yellow silk weaving from Asia Minor, No. 1277.–1888, which is probably of 7th century work.

CLOTH (fragment of) of fine linen, with two bands of woven tapestry, coloured silk. A Kufic inscription runs along both sides of the wider band, one of them is, "In the name of God, " the Merciful, the Gracious. There is no God but God. " Mohammed is the Apostle of God. Ali is the favourite " friend of God" the other is "Al Mustansir billah, Prince " of the Faithful, the blessings of God be upon him, upon his " fathers, the pure Imams and upon his sons." (Al Mustansir billah was living in A.D. 1087.) The main pattern of wider band, with that of the second band below, consists of repeated lozenge shapes, enclosing a four-petalled device. From ancient tombs at Erment, Upper Egypt. ? Saracenic. 11th cent.ʸ. About 19 in. by 7 in. Bought, 10s.   1381.–1888.

Mr. Henry C. Kay discovered sculptured Kufic inscriptions upon the frieze of the Gate, known by the name of Bab-en Nasr at Cairo, and upon the mosque and tomb of Sayyidah Nafisah at Cairo, on which occurs the name of Al Mustansir-billah. (See pamphlet "Inscriptions at Cairo," &c. by Henry C. Kay, M.R.A.S. [From the Journal of the Royal Asiatic Society of Great Britain and Ireland, Vol. XVIII. Part I.]

CLOTH (fragment of) of fine linen, with two similar bands of woven tapestry, coloured silks, chiefly yellow, blue, and red, on fine flax warps.* The pattern of the bands consists of a double intertwining waved stem, forming a succession of small spaces in which are debased renderings ? of floral or leaf devices; this arrangement is bordered on each side with a narrow red stripe with repeated stem and leaf devices. Sham inscriptions are traceable in this specimen. From ancient tombs at Meshaieh, near Girgeh, Upper Egypt. Saracenic. 7th to 11th cent.ʸ 8 in. by 6¾ in. Bought, 1l. 10s.   244.–1890.

* The Arab writer Mukaddasi (10th cent.ʸ) writes " From Palestine come stuffs of mixed silk and cotton."

CLOTH (fragment of) of fine linen, with two bands of woven
tapestry, red, yellow, green, and black silk, on fine flax warps.
The pattern of the upper band consists of a series of oval
spaces filled in with rude renderings of birds and animals,
and set between two narrow stripes of red with repeated stem
and leaf device. The lower band is similar to the first, but
without the narrow red stripe on each side of it. Between
the oval spaces in each band are indications of trefoil devices
in black. Sham inscriptions are traceable in this specimen.
Saracenic. 7th to 11th cent^y. 8¾ in. by 8 in. Bought,
1*l.* 10*s.*   245.-1890.

CLOTH (two fragments of) of fine linen, with bands of woven
tapestry, coloured silks. The wider band consists of a central
arrangement, on a yellow and blue ground, of small roundels,
alternately containing birds and formal floral ornament; on
each side of this, on black ground, are sham inscriptions in
white, and beyond these on blue, in black outline, and red
spots is the wave pattern. From ancient tombs at Meshaieh,
near Girgeh, Upper Egypt. *Saracenic.* 7th to 11th cent^y.
246, 8¼ in. by 7¼ in.; 246*a*, 9½ in. by 4 in. Bought, 3*l.* the
two.   246, 246*a*.-1890.

CLOTH (fragment of) of fine linen, with portions of two bands
of woven tapestry, blue, yellow, and black silk on fine flax
warps. One of the bands is edged on each side with a sham
inscription; the other contains a similar sham inscription
intermingled with blue archaic forms. From ancient tombs
at Meshaieh, near Girgeh, Upper Egypt. *Saracenic.* 7th
to 11th cent^y. About 2 ft. by 10 in. Bought, 1*l.* 10*s.*
                                                      260.-1890.

(*k.*) CIRCULAR PANELS for CLOTHS, &c.

ORNAMENT,? for a cloth, of woven tapestry and needlework, dark
purple wool and white flax. In the centre, on a circular white
ground, is a human head surrounded by four amphora-shaped
vases, alternated with four other forms. The circular border to
the whole is of guilloche ornament outlined with the needle.
On two opposite outer parts of this border are interlaced stem
devices, terminated by a small stem with trefoil ornament.
From ancient tombs at Akhmîm (Panopolis), Upper Egypt.
? *Egypto-Roman.* ? 1st to 6th cent^y. Diam. 8¼ in. Bought,
1*l.* 10*s.*   277.-1889.

MEDALLION (? for a linen robe or cloth) of woven tapestry and
needlework, purple-brown wool and yellow flax. An interlacing narrow band pattern fills the central ground, which is
bordered with a circular band containing alternations of S
devices and small circular devices. From an ancient Roman
cemetery in the Fayûm, Middle Egypt. ? 3rd to 6th cent^y.
H. 11½ in., W. 9½ in. Bought, 1*l.*   461.-1889.

48

POINTED OVAL ORNAMENT of woven tapestry in purple, green, and red wools and yellow flax, for a linen cloth or robe. From a small two-handled amphora-shaped vase (lower part destroyed) springs a tree, amidst the symmetrically arranged branches of which are birds, half boars, a lion, an ibex or goat, and in the centre a nude human figure. From ancient tombs at Akhmîm (Panopolis), Upper Egypt. *Egypto-Roman.* ? 3rd to 9th cent^y. 9½ in. by 9½ in. Bought, 2*l*. 2*s*. 1261.–1888.

This is an extension of the more simple treatment of such ornaments as seen in Nos. 1263.–1888 and 688.–1886.

POINTED OVAL ORNAMENTS of woven tapestry in brown, red, and green wools and yellow flax, for a linen cloth or robe. From a two-handled amphora-shaped vase springs a vine, amongst the symmetrically arranged branches of which are a nude human figure* and two birds (? red-legged partridges); these latter one on each side above the mouth of the vase, which is ornamented with a green band bearing white discs. From ancient tombs at Ahkmîm (Panopolis), Upper Egypt. ? *Egypto-Roman.* ? 3rd to 9th cent^y. About 13 in. by 11 in. Bought, 2*l*. 1263.–1888.

* Amongst Egyptian wall paintings, as at Beni Hassan (2000 B.C.), are paintings of trees formally-shaped, as this vine, in which are monkeys picking fruit.

EIGHT-POINTED STAR-SHAPED ORNAMENT (for a linen cloth or robe), with trefoil terminated stem, of woven tapestry and needlework, dark blue wool and yellow flax. Within the star shape are radiating groups of a vine leaf and two bunches of grapes, set about a central medallion, the ground of which is outlined with a diaper pattern of squares containing looped stems. From ancient tombs at Akhmîm (Panopolis), Upper Egypt. ? 3rd to 9th cent^y. 22 in. by 15½ in. Bought, 10s.
1305.–1888.

Compare triple grape bunch ornament in 804 and 766.–1886, and similar device in 768.–1886.

MEDALLION or CIRCULAR PANEL (for a cloth ?) of woven tapestry and needlework, brown wool and white flax. On a brown roundel in the centre is a yellow bird; this is enclosed within a star device which spreads into an orderly arrangement of crossing stems terminated with vine leaves. The whole is surrounded by a circular band of guilloche pattern outlined in white thread on brown wool. From ancient tombs at Akhmîm (Panopolis), Upper Egypt. ? 3rd to 9th cent^y. Diam. 10 in. Bought, 7s. 6d. 1318.–1888.

ORNAMENT (two pieces joined together, for a cloth ?) of woven tapestry and needlework, purple-black wool and yellow flax. This consists of a scalloped oval shape, having extensions at opposite ends of a triple leaf device, from which there is a narrow stem terminating in a leaf and double scroll device; the stem has on it a circular blossom device. The pattern in the large scallop oval consists of a diaper of squares, diamonds, and circles done in outline in flax. From ancient tombs at Akhmîm (Panopolis), Upper Egypt. ? 3rd to 9th cent^y. Entire L. 2 ft. 1 in., W. 8½ in. Bought, 7s. 6d.
1322, 1322a.–1888.

MEDALLION or CIRCULAR PANEL (for a cloth?) of woven tapestry, brown wool and white flax. The pattern consists of an orderly arrangement of brown triple leaf branches on a white ground, surrounded by a series of brown roundels, each containing a white indented diamond form with brown centre. From ancient tombs at Akhmîm (Panopolis), Upper Egypt. ? 3rd to 9th cent^y. Diam. 9 in. Bought, 1*l.* 274.-1889.

POINTED OVAL ORNAMENT of woven tapestry, dark blue wool filled in with yellowish flax. From a very small amphora-shaped vase springs a vine, with a nude female figure, and birds pecking at the grapes, among its branches. This ornament has been sewn to a piece of linen for the sake of preservation. From ancient tombs at Akhmîm (Panopolis), Upper Egypt. *Egypto-Roman.* ? 3rd to 6th cent^y. 15 in. by 9 in. Bought, 1*l.* 5*s.* 253.-1890.

Compare also with similar ornament, Nos. 1263.-1888, 1261.-1888, 688.-1886.

MEDALLION or CIRCULAR PANEL (for a cloth?) of woven tapestry and needlework, purple wool and white flax thread. The ornament, in outline, consists of a balanced scheme of twisted and interscrolling stems set within a star form, which is surrounded by a band of repeated double scroll devices. From ancient tombs at Akhmîm (Panopolis), Upper Egypt. ? 6th to 9th cent^y. Diam. 14 in. Bought, 13*s.* 365.-1887.

MEDALLION (fragment of) for a linen cloth, of woven tapestry and needlework, purple wool and white flax. The surrounding border consisted of two intertwisted waved stems, one plain, one with circles on it; the main ground covered with an outline pattern of interlacing square and circular devices. This medallion originally was 67½ inches in circumference. From ancient tombs at Akhmîm (Panopolis), Upper Egypt. ? 6th to 9th cent^y. About 19 in. by 12 in. Bought, 5*s.* 1342.-1888.

(*l.*) MATS or ENDS of CLOTHS.

MAT or square panel—a fragment of the inner portion—of woven tapestry and needlework, coloured wool and white flax thread. The ornament seems to have consisted of four linked roundels, in each of which was either a flowering plant (? a rose) or some other device. From ancient tombs at Akhmîm (Panopolis), Upper Egypt. *Egypto-Roman.* 1st to 6th cent^y. About 6 in. by 4 in. Bought, 7*s.* 6*d.* 1326.-1888.

The flowering plant (? rose) is remarkable for its colouring and design.

MAT (or square panel, fragmentary, for a cloth) of woven tapestry, coloured wools and white flax. The border consisted of acanthus leaf scroll, with birds, fruits, and blossoms in between the scrolls, on a white ground. The main portion within the border has a yellow ground covered with four linked roundels, in each of which is either a dog or a basket of fruit; in the centre a foliated cross. From ancient tombs at Akhmîm (Panopolis), Upper Egypt. *Egypto-Roman.* 1st to 6th cent[v] About 10 in. by 7 in. Bought, 7s. 6d. 1328.-1888.

MAT, or end of a cloth of rough towel material, with a square panel of woven tapestry, coloured wool and white flax. In the central medallion is a mounted archer, beneath the legs of his prancing horse a long-eared dog. At each corner of the square is a smaller roundel; two at opposite corners; each contains a little kneeling figure, one with a duck and the other with a hare or long-eared dog; the other two roundels each contains a little kneeling figure, helmeted, and bearing a circular shield, both apparently in the act of throwing. Between the medallions are baskets containing fruit? From ancient tombs at Akhmîm (Panopolis), Upper Egypt. *Egypto-Roman.* ? 1st to 6th cent[y]. 18 in. square. Bought, 2l. 5s. 1260.-1888.

The treatment of the figures and gestures is remarkable. See also note to 892.-1886, Catalogue, p. 79.

MAT, or square for a cloth (fragment of the border only), of woven tapestry, coloured wools and flax thread. The pattern consisted of a series of linked roundels, in each of which was either a basket and fruit or some animal form. From ancient tombs at Akhmîm (Panopolis), Upper Egypt. ? *Egypto-Roman.* 1st to 6th cent[y]. 8 in. by 3 in. Bought, 5s. 304.-1889.

See similar borders in intact mats or squares, such as 745 and 746.-1886.

MAT or end of a cloth of rough towel material, with fragment of a square panel of woven tapestry, coloured wools and white flax. In the centre is a roundel with bird, and at opposite corners were four roundels (two only remaining), within which was either a dog or a lion; between these and radiating from the centre were four green amphora-shape vases with balanced foliated stems coming from them. The enclosing square border consisted of a series of ovals containing dogs or hares. From ancient tombs at Akhmîm Panopolis), Upper Egypt. *Egypto-Roman.* ? 3rd to 6th cent[y]. 16 in. by 14 in. Bought (242 to 297, 29l. 9s. 6d.). 242.-1887.

MAT or end of cloth of rough towel material, with square of woven tapestry, coloured wool and white flax. In central roundel is a red-legged partridge (see also No. 1265.-1888) with leafy spray. In each of the four roundels in the corners is a fish-tailed monster; apparently the emblems of the Evangelists: the bull (St. Luke), the lion (St. Mark), the eagle (St. John), and ? a dog for St. Matthew. Between these are classic-shaped baskets of fruit. From ancient tombs at Akhmîm (Panopolis), Upper Egypt. *Egypto-Roman (Christian).* ? 3rd to 6th cent[y]. 17½ in. square. Bought, 2l. 1266.-1888.

Pagan fish-tailed monsters of similar treatment to those in this specimen may be seen in No. 690.-1886. The emblem for St. Matthew is a man's head (according to St. Jerome), elsewhere it is an angel. St. Augustine held that the lion symbolised St. Matthew, and the man's head, or angel, St. Mark. From the point of view of Christian iconography this specimen has considerable interest. The earliest known emblems of the Evangelists St. Luke and St. Matthew are represented in a terra cotta relief from the Catacombs of the 5th or 6th century ; but, according to authorities, a complete series of the Evangelists does not appear amongst the ornamental subjects of the Catacombs, although the representation of the Evangelists in their human form dates as early as the 5th century.

MAT or end of a cloth of rough towel material, with square of woven tapestry, coloured wool and white flax, enclosing a jewelled cross (pattée), with four ducks (in pairs confronting one another) between the limbs. From ancient tombs at Akhmîm (Panopolis), Upper Egypt. *Christian Coptic.* 4th to 6th cent. 13½ in. square. Bought, 1l. 10s. 1270.–1888.

See also crosses in Nos. 349.–1887, 245.–1887, 1262.–1888, and 296.–1889.

(m.) CLOTHS or HANGINGS EMBROIDERED WITH LOOPED TUFTS OF COLOURED WOOLS.

CLOTH (part of) of rough towel material (*kaunakes* or *gausapum*) with part of a large roundel containing part of a female figure with earring and necklace, and bearing a jug with a handle in her right hand (? Hebe) worked with the needle in looped tufts with coloured wools. The ground of the roundel was originally filled in with brown tufts spotted with small square groups of flax tufts. From ancient tombs at Akhmîm (Panopolis), Upper Egypt. ? 1st to 6th cent. 17½ in. square. Bought, 2l. 280.–1889.

An important example of figure composition worked in this class of embroidery, representing two cupids in a boat, surrounded by a framing of overlapping leaves, is in the British Museum. It appears to date from the 3rd century. Flavius Vopiscus, writing of the Emperor Carinus, says, "Why should I mention the linen cloths brought from Egypt prized on account of their laboured embroidery ? "

CLOTH (part of) of rough towel material, faced with looped linen tufts with portion of a band of woven tapestry and needlework, purple and yellow wool and white flax. Along the band is a guilloche pattern in outline, bordered on each side with linked roundels each containing a leaf device. At the end of the band is a human face surmounted by a yellow head-band with pendent earrings. From ancient tombs at Akhmîm (Panopolis), Upper Egypt. ? 3rd to 6th cent. 11 in. by 4¾ in. Bought (242 to 297, 29l. 9s. 6d.). 254.–1887.

CLOTH or HANGING (portion of) of rough towel material, partly faced with looped linen tufts and partly worked with the needle in tufts of coloured wool. The ornament consists of various bands and a dolphin. On the lower fragment is a human head. From an ancient Roman cemetery in Fayûm, Middle Egypt. ? 3rd to 6th cent. 2 ft. 10 in. by 20 in. Given by H. M. Kennard, Esq. 319.–1888.

HANGING (or cloth) portion of, of rough towel material, worked in needlework with purple wool in tufts or loops with intercrossed rectangular device and narrow bordering. From ancient tombs at Akhmîm (Panopolis), Upper Egypt. ? 3rd to 6th cent?. 3 ft. 5 in. by 2 ft. 11 in. Bought, 1*l*.

283.-1889.

HANGING or CLOTH of rough towel material, linen faced, with looped tufts of flax thread and worked with the needle with purple wool in looped tufts. The ornament consists of a large roundel containing a sort of star device with circular spots and scrolls between its points, in the centre; at opposite corners are four roundels each within a broad right angle ornament; these angle ornaments, curved at each of their ends, are connected together by linking devices at the centre of each series of links is a small star or looped square panel. Above and below the entire ornamental arrangement are double bands with wave pattern edges; the cloth is fringed at two opposite sides. From ancient tombs at Akhmîm (Panopolis), Upper Egypt. ? *Egypto-Roman*. 3rd to 6th cent?. L. 9 ft. 6 in., W. 6 ft.3 in. Bought, 40*l*. 438.-1889.

The double bands are similar in design to smaller bands, No. 720.-1886, and to those on a figure of a veiled woman praying with uplifted hands with an inscription "Dionysas in pace," as displayed in a Roman catacomb painting of the 3rd century. (See Perret's " *Catacombes de Rome*," plate 49, vol. 1).

HANGING or CLOTH (part of) of linen rough towel material worked with the needle with brown wool in looped tufts, with a roundel or medallion containing a square with loops on the sides, and two narrow bands of leaf and stem device repeated. From ancient tombs at Akhmîm (Panopolis), Upper Egypt. ? *Egypto-Roman*. 4th to 6th cent? 2 ft. 9½ in. by 2 ft. 5¼ in. Bought, 1*l*. 10*s*. 362.-1887.

CLOTH (part of) of rough towel material, faced with looped linen threads in tufts, with fragments of a band and a circular parti-coloured device of blue and red worsted in tufts worked with a needle. Below this are six small parallel reeds united and covered with coloured wool? apparently suggesting how the looped work could be done if worked on a foundation of linen or other material. From ancient tombs at Akhmîm (Panopolis), Upper Egypt. 3rd to 9th cent?. 24 in. by 15 in., the fragment, L. 6¾. Bought (with 107, 108), 25*l*. 109, 109*a*.-1887.

PORTION of a cloth of coarse linen worked with the needle in looped tufts with coloured wools. Beneath a twisted band of various colours is a roundel containing a human face set in a jewelled circle, to the right are the remains of a square with a cross inside it. From ancient tombs at Akhmîm (Panopolis), Upper Egypt. 3rd to 9th cent?. 23 in. by 17½ in. Bought, 1*l*. 10*s*. 1269.-1888.

ORNAMENT for a robe of linen, a circular or blossom device worked with the needle in looped tufts with coloured wools. From ancient tombs at Akhmím (Panopolis), Upper Egypt. ? 3rd to 9th centy. 8 in. by 6 in. Bought, 7s. 1336.-1888.

ORNAMENT for a robe of coarse linen, a badge consisting of two brown oblongs joined by a smaller yellow oblong; worked with the needle in looped tufts with brown and yellow wool From ancient tombs at Akhmím (Panopolis), Upper Egypt. ? 3rd to 9th centy. 10 in. by 9 in. Bought, 4s.
1364.-1888.
Compare with similarly shaped badge, No. 1365.-1888.

CLOTH (part of) of linen, worked with the needle with coloured wools in looped tufts. The ornament consists of a rectangular corner band with twisted stem device on it; within the corner is a rose blossom. From ancient tombs at Akhmím (Panopolis), Upper Egypt. ? 3rd to 9th centy. 14½ in. by 12½ in. Bought, 1l. 10s. 281.-1889.

(n.) EMBROIDERY in coloured wools, chiefly in running stitches.

FRAGMENT of brown linen, with an ornament worked in needle-work (short stitches) in blue and red wool and a fringe at one end. From an ancient Roman cemetery in the Fayûm, Middle Egpyt. ? 1st to 6th centy. 12 in. by 7½ in. Given by H. M. Kennard, Esq. 419.-1889.

SQUARE PANEL (from a child's linen robe) embroidered in long and short stitches with brown wool on linen, with an amphora-shape vase, from the handles of which depend vine leaves, one on each side of the base. From ancient tombs at Akhmím (Panopolis), Upper Egypt. ? Egypto-Roman. 3rd to 6th centy. 3 in. by 2½ in. Bought, 1s. 6d. 1379.-1888.
This is especially interesting as an early specimen apparently of Roman embroidery with the needle.

SQUARE PANEL (from a child's linen robe) embroidered in long and short stitches with brown wool on linen, with an amphora-shaped vase, from the handles of which depend vine leaves, one on each side of the base. From ancient tombs at Akhmím (Panopolis), Upper Egypt. ? Egypto-Roman. 3rd to 6th centy. 2 in. square. Bought, 1s. 6d. 1380.-1888.
This is especially interesting as an early specimen apparently of Roman embroidery with the needle.

MEDALLION or CIRCULAR PANEL (for a tunic ?) of woven linen embroidered in a sort of long, short, and twisted stem stitch with coloured wool, with a red and green leafy wreath enclosing a jewelled cross with chain and pendent jewels; on either side of the lower limb of this cross is a dove. From ancient tombs at Akhmím (Panopolis), Upper Egypt. ? 4th or 5th centy. Diam. 8 in. Bought, 2l. 1262.-1888.
Jewelled crosses within wreaths are common devices of the later Roman carved ivory diptychs. This piece, however, is remarkable as an early bit of embroidery.

CLOTH of linen with small squares arranged to form a trellis
pattern and cross or blossom devices within the diamond
spaces, embroidered in coloured wool in a running or short
stitch. The cloth is surrounded by a border of similar
ornament. From ancient tombs at Akhmîm (Panopolis),
Upper Egypt. ? 6th to 9th cent^y. 3 ft. 6 in. by 2 ft. 11 in.
Bought (242 to 297, 29l. 9s. 6d.). 284.–1887.

FRAGMENT of linen, to which is attached a woven band with a
pattern of repeated small ornament worked with a needle in
coloured wool. From ancient tombs at Akhmîm (Panopolis),
Upper Egypt. ? 6th to 9th cent^y. 8½ in. by 1¾ in. Bought
(242 to 297, 29l. 9s. 6d.). 295.–1887.

BAND (for a linen robe) worked in coloured worsted with the
needle in short or running stitches, with a lozenge pattern
and a lozenge-shaped pendant. From ancient tombs at Akhmîm (Panopolis), Upper Egypt. 6th to 9th cent^y 15 in. by
5 in. Bought (349 to 358, 100l.). 353.–1887.

BAND (for a linen robe) worked in coloured worsted with the
needle in short or running stitches, with a lozenge pattern
and a lozenge-shaped pendant. From ancient tombs at Akhmîm (Panopolis), Upper Egypt. 6th to 9th cent^y. 14½ in.
by 4¼ in. Bought (349 to 358, 100l.). 354.–1887.

BAND (? for a cloth of linen) worked with a diaper lozenge
pattern in coloured worsted with the needle in a running
stitch. From ancient tombs at Akhmîm (Panopolis), Upper
Egypt. 6th to 9th cent^y. 16 in. by 3¼ in. Bought (349 to
358, 100l.). 356.–1887.

FRAGMENT of brown linen, worked with the needle in purple
worsted in a running stitch, with figure of a dog? From
ancient tombs at Akhmîm (Panopolis), Upper Egypt. 6th to
9th cent^y. About 6 in. by 4 in. Bought (349 to 358, 100l.).
357.–1887.

FRAGMENT of brown linen, worked with the needle with purple
and yellow wool in a running stitch with the figure of a bird.
From ancient tombs at Akhmîm (Panopolis), Upper Egypt.
6th to 9th cent^y. About 5 in. by 4 in. Bought (349 to 358,
100l.). 358.–1887.

CLOTH (part of) of woven flax with two blue stripes, between
which on a white intervening band are irregular crosses or
stars worked in needlework with blue worsted. From ancient
tombs at Akhmîm (Panopolis), Upper Egypt. 6th to 9th cent^y.
4 ft. 10 in. by 9 in. Bought, 10s. 285.–1889.

FRAGMENT of linen, embroidered in long, short, and satin stitches
with blue, red, and purple wool. The portions of embroidered
patterns are of various sizes; the larger one consisting of a
triangular grouping of heart shapes, within which are trefoil
devices. From an ancient Roman cemetery in the Fayûm,
Middle Egypt. ? 6th to 9th cent^y. 9 in. by 7½ in. Given by
H. M. Kennard, Esq. 320.–1889.

COVER or HANGING (part of) of linen, embroidered in a darning
or running stitch with a trellis pattern in blue wool. From
an ancient Roman cemetery in the Fayûm, Middle Egypt.
? 6th to 9th cent⁷. Irregular shape and size. Given by H. M.
Kennard, Esq. 417.-1889.

FRAGMENT of canvas; of which a portion is embroidered in
darning stitches with brown wool with a diaper pattern
enclosing dots, surrounded by a line of green wool; on another
portion is a stripe of similar embroidery in green and light
red wools. From Dayr Mar Girgis, above Howaweesh, Upper
Egypt. ? 6th to 9th cent⁷. 10 in. by 7 in. Bought, 2s.
247.-1890.

BAND (part of) for a linen robe, embroidered with blue silk in
satin stitch and with black silk in short stitches and open
work. The pattern consists of a series of squares alternately
set with eight-pointed stars and lozenge shapes. From ancient
tombs at Akhmîm (Panopolis), Upper Egypt. ? Saracenic.
7th to 11th cent⁷. 9¾ in. by 8 in. Bought, 7s. 6d.
1320.-1888.

The open work consists of pin holes, the threads about which are whipped with
white silk; and is especially interesting as apparently one of the earliest examples
extant of such work, which was developed some centuries later by the workers in
Persia and the Grecian Archipelago.

CUSHION COVER (?) of coarse linen, embroidered in chain stitches
with coloured silks, with two bands of ? inscriptions and a
smaller one of smaller circles and dots. From ancient tombs
at Akhmîm (Panopolis), Upper Egypt. ? 7th to 11th cent⁷
17 in. square. Bought, 7s. 1330.-1888.
See similar needlework in No. 252.-1890.

BANDS (a pair for a linen robe) of fine canvas, embroidered with
coloured threads (? wool) in irregular long and short stitches.
The pattern, outlined in fine black thread, consists of repetitions of scrolls and leaf devices. From ancient tombs at
Akhmîm (Panopolis), Upper Egypt. ? Saracenic. 7th to
11th cent⁷. Each 9½ in. by 1¼ in. Bought, 5s.
1346, 1346a.-1888.

FRAGMENTS (four) of linen, embroidered, with narrow stripe of
S devices alternated with looped devices in squares, with blue
silk, in small short stitches. From ancient tombs at Akhmîm
(Panopolis), Upper Egypt. ? Saracenic. ? 7th to 11th cent⁷.
Various sizes. Bought, 2s. 1377 to 1377c.-1888.
See similar pattern and work in No. 260.-1889.

FRAGMENT of linen with remnants of short-stitch embroidery in
brown wool, the ornament consisting of a series of little sprigs
or animal devices sprinkled in an orderly distribution over
the ground. From ancient tombs at Erment, Upper Egypt.
Saracenic. ? 7th to 11th cent⁷. About 7½ in. by 4½ in.
Given by the Rev. Greville J. Chester. 1655.-1888.

FRAGMENTS (two) of linen, embroidered in short satin stitch with black wool, each with ornamental border either of repeated lozenge and square devices or of repeated zigzag and square ornament. From ancient tombs at Erment, Upper Egypt. ? *Saracenic.* ? 7th to 11th cent^y. Various sizes. Given by the Rev. Greville J. Chester. 1668, 1668a.–1888.

FRAGMENT of glazed canvas, embroidered with crimson silk in short stitches with a line of Arab inscription. From ancient tombs at Akhmîm (Panopolis), Upper Egypt. *Saracenic.* ? 7th to 11th cent^y. 6½ in. by 3¼ in. Given by the Rev. Greville J. Chester. 257.–1889.

FRAGMENT of linen, embroidered narrow stripe of S devices alternated with looped devices in squares, with blue silk, in small short stitches. From Erment, Egypt. ? *Saracenic.* 7th to 11th cent^y. L. 2 ft. 3 in. Given by the Rev. Greville J. Chester. 260.–1889.

BAND (portion of) for a linen robe, embroidered with blue, green, and brown silks in irregular short and long stitches with a repeated star device. From ancient tombs at Mataieh, Upper Egypt. *Saracenic.* 7th to 11th cent^y. L. 13¼ in., W. 1¾ in. Given by the Rev. Greville J. Chester. 218.–1890.

FRAGMENT of linen, embroidered with blue silks in short satin stitches with three rows of inscriptions (?). From ancient tombs at Meshaieh, near Girgeh, Upper Egypt. *Saracenic.* 7th to 11th cent^y. 8 in. by 3¼ in. Bought, 3s. 6d. 250.–1890.

PORTION OF A LINEN GARMENT? embroidered with coloured silks in long and short and chain stitches with two horizontal bands of crosses and geometrical ornament, one of which is bordered on each side by a row of palm trees with pairs of birds at the trunk of each alternate tree. Between and beyond these horizontal bands are various scattered devices, such as pairs of crowned figures seated, peacocks, other smaller birds, lions, crosses, leaves, and triangular emblems. Towards the lower part are three roundels with borders of apparently sham Kufic inscription. From ancient tombs at Meshaieh, near Girgeh, Upper Egypt. *Christian Coptic.* ? 7th to 11th cent^y. 23 in. by 17½ in. Bought, 5l. 252.–1890.

CUFF, band for a, of embroidery in cross and tent stitches with red and blue silk on linen. The ornament consists of squares and oblongs arranged in parallel series and filled in with small squared and diagonal devices. From ancient tombs at Akhmîm (Panopolis), Upper Egypt. *Arabian.* ? 7th to 11th cent^y. 6 in. by 4½ in. Given by the Rev. Greville J. Chester. 357.–1890.

PORTION OF A LINEN GARMENT with stripes of simple ornament
embroidered with red and black wool in a running stitch.
From ancient tombs at Akhmîm (Panopolis), Upper Egypt.
? *Saracenic.* 9th cent^y. About 2¼ in. square. Bought (242
to 297, 29*l.* 9*s.* 6*d.*). 263.-1887.

PORTION OF A LINEN GARMENT with two bands, one of bird
and one of blossoms in squares embroidered with coloured
wool in a running stitch. From ancient tombs at Akhmîm
(Panopolis), Upper Egypt. ? *Saracenic.* ? 9th cent^y. 14 in.
by 8 in. Bought, 5*s.* 303.-1889.

FRAGMENT of linen, embroidered in short satin stitches with
brown and blue wool, with a small angular ornament terminated at each end with three little leafy stem devices, and
filled in with a lozenge diaper or trellis with ? eagles with
outstretched wings in the lozenge shapes. From ancient
tombs at Akhmîm (Panopolis), Upper Egypt. ? 9th to 12th
cent^y. About 6 in. square. Bought, 5*s.* 1355.-1888.

The devices looking like eagles may be debased leaf forms. The diaper in conjunction with the eagles is a typical pattern of the 11th and later centuries when
diapers and heraldic forms were in vogue.

FRAGMENTS (two) of linen, each embroidered in irregular chain
stitch with red silk with two rows of apparently sham Kufic
inscription. From ancient tombs at Meshaieh, near Girgeh,
Upper Egypt. *Saracenic.* 13th cent^y. 249, 11 in. by 4 in. ;
249*a*, 10 in. by 4 in. Bought, 6*s.* 6*d.* the two.
249, 249*a.*-1890.

(*o.*) BAGS.

BAGS (two portions) of woven tapestry in coloured wool, with
cords for tying. The ornament is of a debased character, and
includes a series of garlands, birds, and baskets of fruit ; also
a dark coloured square with two small rounds within it.
From ancient tombs at Akhmîm (Panopolis), Upper Egypt.
3rd to 9th cent^y. Greatest L. 11 in. Bought 10*s.* the two.
1299, 1299*a.*-1888.

FRAGMENT (probably of a bag) of brown woollen stuff, with
tapestry woven yellow band, on which are represented, in
colours, cupids and figures of birds of degraded type within
linked roundels with alternate blue and faded red grounds.
The details for the most part are outlined in black. From an
ancient Roman cemetery in the Fayûm, Lower Egypt. ? 3rd
to 9th cent^y. 12 in. by 11 in. Bought, 10*s.* 467.-1889.

www.ingramcontent.com/pod-product-compliance
Lightning Source LLC
Chambersburg PA
CBHW021635270326
41931CB00008B/1037